Creative Hospitality

Creative

How to Turn Home Entertaining Into a Real Ministry

Hospitality

Nancy Van Pelt, CFCS

REVIEW AND HERALD® PUBLISHING ASSOCIATION
HAGERSTOWN, MD 21740

Texts credited to NIV are from the *Holy Bible, New International Version.* Copyright © 1973, 1978, 1984, International Bible Society. Used by permission of Zondervan Bible Publishers.

Verses marked TLB are taken from *The Living Bible,* copyright © 1971 by Tyndale House Publishers, Wheaton, Ill. Used by permission.

For information about Creative Hospitality Seminars for your church or women's organization, please contact the author, Nancy Van Pelt, in care of Review and Herald® Publishing Association, P.O. Box 119, Hagerstown, MD 21740.

This book was
Edited by Gerald Wheeler
Designed by Patricia S. Wegh
Cover photo by Joel D. Springer
Illustrations by Mary Bausman
Typeset: 11.5/13.5 Times

PRINTED IN U.S.A.

99 98 97 96 95   10 9 8 7 6 5 4 3 2 1

R&H Cataloging Service
Van Pelt, Nancy Lue
    Creative hospitality: how to turn home
entertaining into a real ministry.

    1. Entertaining.   2. Witness bearing (Christianity).   I. Title.

395.3

ISBN 0-8280-0894-9

DEDICATION

Dedicated to my mother, Elsie M. Reel,
the gracious woman who through example
has taught me the true art of creative hospitality
and who continues to encourage me
in this exciting area of my life.

And to my dear friend and mentor, Dee Machock,
a truly gifted homemaker
who has shared her gift for hospitality
and decorating so freely with me.

And to my partner in many of these adventures,
my husband, Harry,
a superb host,
who has patiently helped me
with these experiments
in entertaining for our Friend Jesus.

CREATIVE *H*OSPITALITY

CONTENTS

CREATIVE HOSPITALITY

CREATIVE HOSPITALITY

In addition to what I learned at home, a gracious Southern lady greatly influenced my family's concept of entertaining, although at the time few of us realized it.

ONE GRAND OPPORTUNITY

I've been attending parties since I was 2 years old. From my earliest childhood I remember parties— good food, games, and music all combined well to entertain our friends. I was born into a family that had a wide circle of friends and loved to entertain. Whatever I've learned about entertaining, I learned there—at home, by example, from two very extraordinary people—Mom and Dad.

Some of my earliest and fondest memories date back to family gatherings. In the years that followed the Great Depression money was tight. Until he started his own business, my father worked hard for a few cents an hour. But on Saturday night he would splurge on a quart of ice cream. Then he would invite friends over to share the ice cream along with some other snacks. The children of our guests would join my sister and me in the upstairs playroom for great fun.

Age 12 marked a dramatic, exciting change in my life when our dad fulfilled a dream by purchasing beachfront property at Brown's Point in Tacoma, Washington. There on one of the most beautiful pieces of property on Puget Sound my dad built a family home. What he couldn't do with his own hands he contracted out. During the two-year building period we lived in a two-car garage while we poured all the family funds and time into building a large and lovely beachfront home. However, my mom and dad did not wait until we had completed our new home to entertain. They entertained with what they had—the garage.

Once we were into our new home on the bay with its fantastic view of Maury Island, Dash Point, passing cargo and naval ships, as well as frequent regattas and stunning sunsets, the hospitality spirit that both my parents had nurtured and practiced for years now became an even greater part of our lives. Our many-windowed "nest" overlooking the comings and goings of the tides, restless waves, and soaring sea gulls provided the perfect atmosphere for social occasions of every kind.

Some of my most delightful memories include music. Although my dad never had the opportunity to take a music lesson in his entire life, the Lord blessed him with genuine talent and appreciation for music. Purely for his own benefit and the enjoyment of friends he played the piano, clarinet, and guitar. I distinctly recall other guests who were accomplished vocalists. Music filled the air of our home. Sometimes the group even recorded their efforts—strictly for their own amusement. After we served a smorgasbord of food in the dining room with its spectacular 90-degree view, guests were offered a great selection of outdoor activities—badminton, tennis, croquet, boating, swimming, waterskiing, and bonfires on the beach, to name a few.

You can make more friends in two months by becoming interested in other people than you can in two years by trying to get other people interested in you.

My mother received endless requests from the church and others to host baby and wedding showers because of the view and location of our home. Even though my father was not a church member, almost every week after church we had company for dinner.

The home in which I grew up greatly influenced my dating

years. Any young man who dated me had better like people and parties, as well as outdoor and water sports! I often describe my teen years as ideal because they involved so many healthful activities. Hanging out in shopping malls had not yet hit the scene, and if it had, my crowd would have been bored with it. We were having too much good clean fun at my house to waste time in malls.

During my junior and senior years of high school, the classes asked to hold their annual events at my home because no one could think of a more perfect place to have fun. Waterskiing, swimming, boating, and then a beautiful evening bonfire on the beach were all memorable ingredients of a class party.

This was the world into which Harry walked the day he entered my life. The Korean War now dominated the world scene. Fort Lewis, located in Tacoma, was the point from which young men embarked for Korea. Many of them attended the Tacoma Central church. My mother and I made it a practice to invite guests home after church. I enjoyed entertaining people of all ages, but they also frequently included people in my own age group—particularly if they were male, tall, and handsome. In order to fulfill our patriotic duty to God and country we frequently invited servicemen over for a home-cooked meal. It provided an opportunity for me to get to know young men from all over the United States—a most interesting and varied dating life, to be sure. My dad complained that he had to feed half of Fort Lewis before he ever got me married off! But that is how I met Harry—the one who came to dinner, and never left.

It is hardly surprising, then, that this same home became the choice for my wedding. The setting provided a phenomenal backdrop. The organ played, and almost 100 of our closest and dearest family members and friends witnessed our wedding in my family home. The dining room, with its picture-perfect view of Puget Sound, provided an ideal location for the reception.

Although this home passed from our family's hands to another family in 1980, I will never forget what I learned about entertaining there. To this day, when I visit my mother in Tacoma, one of the things we enjoy most is driving past the family home my father built at Brown's Point. As we peer over the fence into the house, we fondly remember a time it belonged to us. Oh, the joyous family gatherings and the many fun times that home provided us! It proved to be a blessing to us as well as many others over the 32 years it remained in our family.

In addition to what I learned at home, a gracious Southern lady greatly influenced my family's concept of entertaining, although at the time few of us realized it. It began with my mother, Elsie Carlson-Reel, who was born in Tacoma to immigrant parents from Sweden. My grandparents Ida and Daniel Carlson had three daughters—Ruth, Elsie (my mother), and Pearl. Their little family worked hard to maintain a living on a few acres of ground. Papa Daniel barely made enough as a carpenter at the shipyards to provide for family needs.

One day, while at work at the shipyards, Papa Daniel cut himself. The wound did not heal properly, and in spite of medical attention, it worsened. A large lump with red streaks formed on his arm. The doctors, with their limited knowledge about blood poisoning, cut into his arm, which allowed the blood poisoning to spread. Soon Papa Daniel was dead.

This threw my grandmother and her three girls into real financial deprivation. But as my mother tells me now: "We didn't know we were poor." Other wealthier families helped them from time to time, and they eked out an existence there on their small farm.

As the girls entered their midteens they dreamed of going to college. But tuition was expensive, and how could they ever realize their goal of a college education? The girls hired out to large wealthy homes in the north end of town as housekeepers, or "second girls," as they were known. Second girls prepared and served meals in the elegant dining rooms, cleaned, ironed, polished, and were available to do almost anything asked of them. Carefully supervised and instructed by the mistress of the home, they learned how to do things well. They were present at most, if not all, dinner parties and festive occasions hosted by their wealthy employers—not as guests, but as servants. But it was here, as a servant, that my mother learned expertise in entertaining, as well as social skills that otherwise might not have been available to her.

Another job offer with a little more money came from a nearby wealthy family. My mother soon became a second girl for Nancy Elva Hudson, a delightful, cultured Southern belle from the Deep South. Ms. Hudson had never married, and lived in a three-story-plus-basement Southern mansion. The front porch had mammoth white columns heavily laden with lush wisteria. The house was immense. In addition to a large living room and sitting and dining areas, it had eight bedrooms, sun porches, linen and china closets the size of today's bedrooms, grand stairways, and lavish gardens. All of this took a great deal of care.

It is one of the most beautiful compensations of life that no man can sincerely try to help another without helping himself.

RALPH WALDO EMERSON

At first my mother only assisted with serving Ms. Hudson and her brother each evening as they sat at opposite ends of the long dining table. Soon my mother was working there quite regularly, assisting at elite dinner parties. When Ms. Hudson needed service, she pressed a button strategically positioned under the rug close to where her foot rested. The buzzer sounded in the kitchen. My mother, dressed in a black uniform with white apron and matching white cap, quickly appeared on the scene to attend their every need.

One day the head cook and housekeeper went on vacation . . . and never returned. My mother, who could work only part-time because she attended school full-time, encouraged my grandmother, Ida, to apply for the position. Ida felt terribly inadequate to handle so much responsibility for such an important position. But after much prodding and encouragement from Mom, who promised to show her mother the ropes, Ida eventually took the job.

Ida received her own quarters on the third floor but continued to maintain her own home for the sake of her girls. My mother continued to work there part-time. About this time my mother and father were courting and planning their marriage. Ms. Hudson offered her home as a setting for their wedding. A spacious stairway with an ornate railing led from the second story to a large landing, and then another flight of stairs swept down to an immense foyer and living room on the first floor. There among some of the most expensive, ornate, and elaborate antiques and valuables ever created, my mother and father exchanged their wedding vows.

When I entered the scene a year later I was named Nancy in honor of the very special Nancy Elva Hudson who had so graciously provided her home for my parents' wedding. Some of my earliest memories revolve around this ornately beautiful Southern mansion built in Tacoma to replicate Ms. Hudson's original home in Canton, Mississippi.

Both my mother and grandmother had keys to a side door of Ms. Hudson's home so they could come and go from work as they pleased. But because of the immensity of the home with so many rooms on each level, we never knew where we would find Ms. Hudson. As we entered, my mother and grandmother would call out a friendly greeting to let her know we were there. "Yoo-hoo! Where are you?" I was small and didn't quite understand the procedure and certainly not all the words. I thought that "Yoo-hoo" was her name. Thus it was that Nancy Elva Hudson, this gracious Southern belle who spoke impeccable English with a cultured Southern drawl, became affectionately known to all of us as Hoo Hoo, the closest my baby talk could get to "Yoo-hoo."

My father eventually went to work for her and managed Hudson Machinery, the family business. My mother also worked part-time at the office. And my grandmother continued on as helper and housekeeper. Our families became intricately intertwined. Her home became our second home. I had my own bedroom on the third floor but claimed several others around the house as well. There was the blue room, and the white rooms reserved mostly for guests, but my favorite bedroom by far was a guest room next to Ms. Hudson's private quarters. I loved to drape myself leisurely on the massive and ornately carved canopy bed, the closest thing to being a "princess" that I would ever know! The canopy above was a regal deep rose in color, and the gathers evenly met in the center of the canopy and were held in place by a large button covered in the same fabric.

It was there in that home that I found myself surrounded by many of the finer things in life. Hoo Hoo had a linen and china closet filled with enough fine pieces to supply a modest store. China and crystal fascinated her, so the vast quantities that she had purchased over the years were stored in elegant long glass closets on the second floor.

Christmas always meant exquisite gifts from her. One that I cherish the most and have saved is an exquisite doll that sits on a "Hoo Hoo chair" in my living room today. Ms. Hudson also introduced me to great literature and gave me leatherbound classics. Then she had me read aloud to her, carefully instructing me in pronunciation and grammar and also teaching me clear enunciation and how to read with feeling. I didn't realize it at the time, but she was already preparing me to be a future public speaker. Frequently after I speak today, an older woman will say to me, "Nancy, I'm hard of hearing and so many people mumble when they speak. But when you speak, I can hear every word." Thank you, Hoo Hoo.

Another of my favorite memories includes a special drawer in which she kept special treats for my sister Ginger and me. The treat always included a huge chunk of chocolate from which we'd break off pieces for a special snack. The minute we'd enter the house we'd run for that drawer.

Something else that became almost a Saturday night ritual was a stop at Ms. Hudson's. We'd make yummy sandwiches and drink orange soda. On these occasions she would eat with us around the butcher block table with an assortment of kitchen utensils hanging over our heads. Although we learned so much from her, she too gained much by becoming part of our family.

To her life we added a dimension she never would have known otherwise, and added fun and laughter she would have missed with her more cloistered and elegant style of living. With a little urging from Ginger and me, she would blow marbles or ping-pong balls across her dining room table. Once Ms. Hudson orchestrated a make-believe wedding in an English garden next door. A home movie camera recorded this momentous event in which my sister was the bride and I the bridal attendant. We had no groom, but we didn't need one in those days to pull off fancy-dress childish adventure with style. Hoo Hoo embraced us as her own!

> *The only ones among you who will be really happy are those who have sought and found how to serve.*
> ALBERT SCHWEITZER

From her house I could walk to both my junior and senior high schools. So during those years, especially when I had after-school activities, I stayed at her home. Thus Hoo Hoo's house became a second home, and I spent much of my childhood and growing-up years there. She had many friends but no family. So our family became her family. We took her in as one of us, and she treated us as her family.

As a real Southern lady, she never learned to drive and either had to take taxis wherever she went or have what she wanted delivered. Thus she would plan meals and had the list of groceries called to the local grocer, who would bring them to the house.

When I was 15 my family told me that Hoo Hoo wasn't well and that I could no longer visit her as I once did. Her illness worsened, and within just months our lovely Southern friend was gone.

Yes, she was physically gone, but nothing could steal from us the influence she had had on all of us. We had all become more cultured, refined, and greatly enriched through her gracious and soft-spoken hospitality.

The rich heritage of culture, refinement, and love of beauty she left us lives on in each member of my family. How? My grandmother became so much more than mere hired help or cook and housekeeper to her. Ida became a friend, companion, and confidant. And when Nancy Elva Hudson died, she willed the home and all its beautiful furnishings to my grandmother. Shortly thereafter my grandmother died and left it all to my mother and her two sisters. Some of the finest antique furniture, china, crystal, silver, and other pieces have been lovingly handed down to each new generation with a special request to keep as many of these treasures in the family as possible.

I have pieces of furniture, silver, crystal, and china from Hoo Hoo that are so precious to me that I almost weep as I touch them. And as I serve others with these things that I have inherited from her, I get flashbacks to when I was a child and saw Hoo Hoo entertaining her guests so elegantly. It makes me want to sit a little taller.

What a heritage I have been given. How much I have benefited culturally. How much I learned about serving, table settings, hospitality, and refinement through the chance part-time job my mother accepted at Ms. Hudson's home—a legacy I want to pass on to my children even though our precious Hoo Hoo is long gone. It is a vivid example of how *just one life* can influence so many others in a powerful, positive way! Yet each of us has received the same: one brief life, one grand opportunity.

With such a rich background of entertaining experiences, you may think that it would come easier for me than for you. Yet I have discovered that even those with innate abilities for entertaining must practice and refine their skills. If hospitality is to be more than striking centerpieces and beautiful homes, we must look at the spirit of how we minister to others. To really meet the needs of others we must yield our talents and abilities to the Holy Spirit, asking for His blessings on our efforts.

*Abraham urged his guests
to honor him by coming to his home for refreshments.*

2

BIBLICAL MODELS OF HOSPITALITY

he Bible teaches us to practice hospitality. Paul clearly lists it as a necessary qualification for church elders. "He must be *hospitable*" (Titus 1:8, NIV). *The Living Bible* elaborates on this by saying, "They must enjoy having guests in their homes." Verse 9 combines the word "encouragement" with hospitality: "He must hold firmly to the trustworthy message as it has been taught, so that he can *encourage* others by sound doctrine" (NIV).

Romans 12:9-13 carries the trademark of hospitality beyond elders to all believers: "Love must be sincere. Hate what is evil; cling to what is good. Be devoted to one another in brotherly love. Honor one another above yourselves. Never be lacking in zeal, but keep your spiritual fervor, serving the Lord. Be joyful in hope, patient in affliction, faithful in prayer. Share with God's people who are in need. *Practice hospitality*" (NIV).

The Living Bible throws a little more light on verse 13. "When God's children are in need, you be the one to help them out. And get into the habit of inviting guests home for dinner or, if they need lodging, for the night." The directive is clear: "*practice hospitality.*"

Hospitality Versus Entertainment

The dictionary defines *hospitality* as "the reception and entertainment of guests, or strangers with liberality and kindness." *Entertainment* is an agreeable occupation for the mind—one of "diversity and amusement and generally includes a performance of some kind or the hospitable provision for the wants of guests."

In this book I make no distinction between the two. Scripture uses *entertain*. It is a good word to which some people attach a negative connotation. Hospitality and entertainment can both be positive when the motive is to serve and encourage others.

Sometimes people's motive for entertaining is wrong. We should not do it to impress guests with exquisite table settings and gourmet cooking, or to show off decorator-perfect furnishings. In *The Gracious Woman*, author Jean Curtis recalls advice given the wives of law school graduates by their dean: "To be an asset to your husband's practice, join every organization you can. Entertain as much as possible. It's important to make friends with the right people." Much worldly entertaining has this type of motive. I will ask you to my home and entertain you for certain benefits that may come my way as a result of it.

True hospitality has a different focus. Karen Mains in her book *Open Heart—Open Home* says: "Hospitality, however, seeks to minister. It says, 'This home is not mine. It is truly a gift from my Master. I am His servant and I use it as He desires.' Hospitality does not try to impress, but to serve."*

A loving and encouraging spirit generously offers hospitality. It treats guests graciously, considerately, and kindly and never under duress or grudgingly.

"I hate it when it is my turn to have people over," Sharon muttered under her breath in a barely audible voice. "But I have to do it, so I might as well get it over with so I can stop dreading it." Such an attitude, though, can rob you of a real blessing. "Offer hospitality to one another without grumbling" (1 Peter 4:9). So the spirit in which one extends hospitality becomes important.

The Never-Empty Barrel

Not only does the Bible tell us to be hospitable, but it also provides examples of hospitality. The widow of Zarephath (1 Kings 17:12-24) is one such instance. God sent His hungry servant Elijah to ask for food from a poverty-stricken widow during a time of severe famine. "Would you bring me a little water in a jar so I may have a drink?" he asked. As she was going to get it, he called, "And bring me, please, a piece of bread" (verses 10, 11, NIV).

"As surely as the Lord your God lives," she replied, "I don't have any bread—only a handful of flour in a jar and a little oil in a jug. I am gathering a few sticks to take home and make a meal for myself and my son, that we may eat it—and die" (verse 12, NIV).

Elijah said to her, "Don't be afraid. Go home and do as you have said. But first make a small cake of bread for me from what you have and bring it to me, and then make something for yourself and your son. For this is what the Lord, the God of Israel, says: 'The jar of flour will not be used up and the jug of oil will not run dry until the day the Lord gives rain on the land'" (verses 13, 14, NIV).

At the very time she was about to use up her meager fare a stranger suddenly asked for it. It tested her faith in the power of the living God to the utmost. But in a

Man should not consider his material possessions as his own, but common to all, so as to share them without hesitation when others are in need.
St. Thomas Aquinas

beautiful and generous manner she offered hospitality by sharing what she had with this stranger. And how wonderfully God rewarded her—the flour and meal lasted as long as God said it would. Imagine what fun the angels must have had filling the containers of oil and flour when the widow wasn't looking!

Some time later when the woman's son became extremely ill and stopped breathing, Elijah pleaded to the Lord on behalf of the boy, and the child lived. The widow of Zarephath shared her food with Elijah, and in return God spared her life and that of her son—in fact, God spared the son's life twice. God has offered great blessings to those who freely give kindness to others. And His power is no less now than in the days of Elijah.

God will actually put opportunities in our path so we may *practice hospitality* to others—opportunities that are really blessings in disguise. "And if anyone gives even a cup of cold water to one of these little ones because he is my disciple, I tell you the truth, he will certainly not lose his reward" (Matt. 10:42, NIV). No act of kindness will fail to receive recognition and reward.

Abraham Entertains Angels

Abraham was sitting in the door of his tent one hot summer noontime. As he looked out over the quiet landscape he saw in the distance three travelers approaching. They drew near, stopped, and appeared to be discussing which way to go next. Without waiting for them to ask for any favors, Abraham rose and went toward them. Just as they were apparently turning in another direction, Abraham hurried after them and with great courtesy urged them to honor him by coming to his home for refreshments. Although Abraham was a man of wealth, power, and position, with his own hands he brought them water so they might wash their dusty feet. He himself selected their food.

As the guests awaited the serving of the meal Abraham entertained them. In the days before stereos, compact disks, and music videos, I suspect it may have included musical instruments and singing, a relaxing treat for tired travelers.

Abraham then stood beside his guests while they ate the meal he had selected for them. Perhaps the culture did not permit him to partake with his guests, but he was there to oversee the entire affair and make certain all their needs were cared for. True hospitality plus!

At first Abraham saw his guests only as three tired travelers, but as two of them departed, the Lord revealed Himself to Abraham. It was then that Abraham learned that he had not only entertained angels but had entertained Christ Himself!

The hospitality Abraham extended to these strangers was so important that nearly 2,000 years later Inspiration referred to it: "Do not forget to entertain strangers, for by so doing some people have entertained angels without knowing it" (Heb. 13:2, NIV).

Strangers at the Gate

Abraham's nephew, Lot, also possessed and practiced hospitality. One night, as twilight approached, two strangers approached the city gate. They seemed to be travelers seeking a place to stay for the night. Although Sodom was a city of luxurious semitropical oases, it was also a wicked place in which people openly defied God and engaged in unrestrained violence and brutal passions.

Lot feared for the very lives of these strangers should they enter the city unawares. To protect them from harm, he invited them to his home. He gave little or no thought as to whether the men might harm him or his family. Lot did not know the character or reputation of the men, but hospitality was such a part of his nature that it had become habitual. He had seen the abuse that strangers faced in Sodom and made it one of his duties to guard them.

Observing the two men, he took them home to provide them with food, lodging, and safety. Those involved in the feeding, care, and protection of the homeless, another type of hospitality, might be following in Lot's footsteps.

Mother Teresa rose each morning at 4:30 to minister to the poorest of poor on the sidewalks of Calcutta. This unusual woman heard the call to give up all and follow Him to the slums to serve the less fortunate. Taking a vow of extreme voluntary poverty, she worked among the outcasts of society—the leprous, the orphaned, the beggars, the diseased. She gave love to those awaiting death in the streets in the same way that she would have offered it to her dying Saviour. She enabled these abandoned people to die with dignity. Such radical hospitality serves as an example of the type of hospitality that the church must not neglect.

Teaching family life seminars has taken me to the far corners of the earth and greatly opened my eyes to serving the needs of others. One experience in Cebu City in the Philippines will haunt me forever. A car picked me up at the hotel on the hill where I was being comfortably housed. We arrived at the hotel downtown and someone opened the sliding door of the van for me. As I got out I encountered a child of about 5. A tattered, grimy shirt hung loosely from his thin shoulders. A dirty band-aid stretched across his forehead. He made no sound as his eyes pleaded with mine, only lifting his hand to his mouth in a gesture that he needed something to eat. Although our host quickly shooed him away, those pleading eyes will live with me forever. "I tell you the truth," the Lord replied, "whatever you did for one of the least of these brothers of mine, you did for me" (Matt 25:40, NIV). I wish I could go back and do more for this child.

> *Let us not be satisfied with just giving money. Money is not enough, money can be got, but they need your hearts to love them. So, spread your love everywhere you go.*
> MOTHER TERESA

Christ Feeds a Multitude

Christ also practiced hospitality. He had gone to a secluded place with His disciples for some much-needed rest and relaxation. But before He and His disciples reached the shore, a crowd of 5,000 men plus women and children had already gathered to wait for Him.

After a short rest, He looked for a convenient place where He could minister to the crowd. His healing hands brought life to the dying and health to the ill and suffering. The people listened spellbound when Christ spoke, and forgot how long it had been since they had eaten anything.

Even as the sun set, the people lingered. Christ was now pale from weariness and hunger. The disciples urged Him to send the people away. But Christ knew if He let them go in search for a meal, many would not return. He instructed the disciples to seat the people in groups of 50 or 100 to preserve order and so that all might see what He was about to do. Then He took two small fishes and five barley loaves that a small boy had supplied, blessed them, and asked His disciples to serve the people. The food miraculously multiplied in His hands. The hands of the disciples were never empty as they passed portions to all the people.

Christ had all the resources of heaven at His disposal. He had only to speak the word and a five-course banquet would have instantly appeared. Instead He used His creative power in a different way to satisfy their need for food. The meal was very simple—fish and bread. No luxuries. Simple, everyday food. But by taking care of their hunger, He provided assurance of His love and power, that He personally cared for their everyday needs. And while they ate barley loaves Christ taught them also how to eat of the bread of life.

Christ's example of hospitality provides a tremendous example for us. We may not have luxurious homes in which to entertain, but then neither did Christ. He entertained outdoors. Perhaps we may not have a lavish budget for expensive meals, but then neither did Christ. He served fish and bread. Or we may not have exquisite table decorations. Christ served with no tables at all! Yet we can serve what we do have in love. That's all that God requires of us.

On a cold Thanksgiving many years ago a woman put the finishing touches on a feast she'd been preparing for days. She sent her son to gather the family. When he came back he asked if there was room for one more. A hobo had wandered into their yard from a nearby train depot, and her husband had invited him to stay for dinner.

The stranger joined the others at the table, gobbling down his food as if he hadn't had a meal in days. As the afternoon unfolded, the family discovered that the hobo's wife and children had died in a car crash. They also learned that he used to be a teacher, and that he was very good at magic tricks as he entertained all the children with his surprising talent.

When he departed he thanked the family profusely for their hospitality and asked for their names and address, which he wrote in a notebook. "I'll never forget you for this day," he said.

A year later and every year for 20 years the family received a Thanksgiving card addressed to all the family with a $100 bill enclosed. It was always signed, "Love from Hobo Bob." Could Hobo Bob have been an angel in disguise?

---

*Karen Mains, *Open Heart—Open Home* (Elgin, Ill.: David C. Cook Pub., Inc., 1976), p. 14.

*To know how to create a beautiful table setting
and put it all together in an inviting manner is a talent from God.*

HOSPITALITY:
KEEPING MEMBERS

A series of revival meetings held in the South Valley church received great support from the congregation. They had brought in a guest evangelist from another area. The attendance was excellent, and the congregation rejoiced when over a three-month period 30 people were added to the church. New vitality and enthusiasm flowed through the older members from the addition of the new ones.

The enthusiasm was short-lived, however, and soon the South Valley church returned to its normal activities and status quo. At a board meeting about a year later someone mentioned how the great revival meetings had influenced the church a short year before. Someone else asked where the people were who had joined the church. Checking the records, the board found that only 10 of the original 30 were still attending church. What had happened to the other 20?

New believers often find it difficult to live up to the high standards of the church whose lifestyle may be so different from their previous one. They may also be dealing with relatives who may not understand, let alone approve of, their new lifestyle. As they leave their old life behind and move into a new church family, they may find themselves losing one set of friends and searching for new ones. Since it takes time to establish friendships, this leaves them dangling without a solid support system.

Within a few months such new members often become discouraged. The joy in their newfound life wears thin as they find little tolerance among more established members during their transition period. Criticism of "mistakes" further destroys their confidence in their new faith.

New members will not survive if left alone. Unless they receive adequate attention and begin to bond with members already established in the church, they are at a high risk for dropout. The transitions they are called upon to make during this critical period are difficult. It is especially now that they desperately need friendship.

The Major Crises

One experienced minister reports four major crises occurring in the lives of new believers within the first two years. He names (1) discouragement, (2) integration, (3) lifestyle, and (4) leadership as the major ones they will encounter.[1]

The crisis of integrating into the new community begins when new believers fail to replace old friends with new ones and thus do not become a part of the social network of the church. One study shows new members need to make 8-10 friends in the first nine months of membership or they will drop out.[2] They often feel alone and isolated, even from their own families, because of their new commitment.

It is in the shelter of each other that the people live.
IRISH PROVERB

Symptoms that indicate new converts are on their way out begin with haphazard attendance, arriving late for church, or leaving immediately after the worship service without attempting to visit with others. Potential dropouts sit by themselves, keep to themselves, and rarely or never attend social functions.

To such persons, religion has become little more than attending their new church's worship service because they have been convicted of the doctrines. But they have little association with church members and they have no close friends. This may go on for some time, but sooner or later, unless they develop a social network of friends, they will drop out.

Every congregation must give immediate personal attention to such members in order to help them establish friendships. They should be invited to all church social functions. But this needs to be taken a step further. New members need invitations into our homes, to have extended to them personal friendship and hospitality. Only in this way can believers *see* how Christians live rather than only hearing about it or having it preached to them.

How to Cut the Dropout Rate

If every established church member would offer friendship and hospitality to a new member, we could cut the dropout rate to near zero. I encourage those who habitually get together with friends to open their circle to include one or two more. This is more difficult than it appears on the surface, however. If you have a group of people you click with, it can be very threatening to ask others to join you. The new members could take *your* friends away, disrupt a good thing, or in other ways sabotage your friendships. But it is worth the risk. Unless we do this, unless we begin to open up to new converts, we will continue to have a staggering dropout rate.

One of the most pleasant ways of extending friendship is to invite new members to your home. When asking friends over for dinner after church, invite several new members also. If you are getting together for pizza on a Saturday night, ask a new family to join you. Or if you are going for a picnic in the park, encourage a new member to join you. Think of it this way: *Every time you plan any type of social get-together with friends, open up your circle to include someone new.*

Especially do new converts need to be invited into your home. It is here, as you engage in casual and relaxed conversation, that you will really get to know their hearts and respond to what they feel are their needs. Only here will you be able to minister to their social needs through warm, loving fellowship. The deep personal relationships developed over your dining room table can do a lot to prevent apostasy in the church among new believers.

Hospitality and Established Members

Most of us tend to believe that the typical drop-out is a blue-collar worker brought into the church through a short evangelistic campaign. He caves in when he faces pressure. Or she may be a poorly educated woman who after a few quick Bible studies is taken into church membership but is unable to quit smoking. Research into the dropout problem gives an entirely different picture, however.

The typical dropout grew up in the faith, is a young adult (half of all dropouts are 20 to 35 years of age), and has gone through a divorce or has never married. Research identifies members of this group as *having few friends in his or her local church,* holding a professional position or white-collar job, and finding that the local church program does not meet his or her needs.

Evidence points to the fact that the underlying cause for their leaving the church is that they *never bonded with the core group of their congregation, never felt a part of the "inner circle."* They also report few visits or contacts by the pastor or other members while a part of the congregation. This group leaves the church, not because they no longer believe the doctrines, but because they never made friends. Established members failed to reach out in friendship or include them in any social get-togethers. A letter I received from someone attending my Creative Hospitality Seminar pretty well sums it up:

"I have attended the city church for five years, and to this date no one ever spoke to me or, heaven forbid, ever asked my husband and me to their homes or gatherings. On several occasions I tried to initiate conversations with people, but I was ignored as if I was thin air. I have been a member of two other churches in my life. These churches were responsive and warm, and I held many church offices, including social director and hospitality coordinator, and I never had this problem.

"I am a professional in the city, and since November of last year have not attended the city church or any other church because of the nonhappening I found so evident in the church. I find it a real burden to sit in a cold tomb week after week. Now I have chosen to build a wall of hard cement so as not to feel the intense pain

> *It is the first law of friendship that it has to be cultivated. The second is to be indulgent when the first law is neglected.*
> VOLTAIRE

that has resulted. I am a friendly and intelligent person who will survive without my church, since I have friendships outside the church. It is time you and others start practicing what you preach. If you are going to preach hospitality, I suggest you practice it."

Was the problem found with the church? individual members? or her?

A friend's husband was being transferred to a new area. They had just bought a home and had it decorated and finished the way they wanted it. She didn't want to move and was angry, upset, and very resentful about the move. While house hunting in the new area, she and her husband attended church. Inwardly what she really wanted was for the new church to show her they were a warm and friendly place. Outwardly she took her I-don't-want-to-be-here feelings to church along with a chip on her shoulder.

The greeter at the door welcomed them and asked where they were visiting from. Although someone gave them a bulletin, no one offered them a dinner invitation or welcome of any other kind. So naturally she concluded it was not a warm and friendly place. She had known she was going to hate it there, and now she did.

But before the move took place she recognized that she needed to make an attitude adjustment—*her attitude toward the church.* The next time she went to the church she determined to go in there smiling and say hello to everyone, rather than just waiting for someone else to approach her and say hello. As a result she left the church that day feeling it was a much warmer and friendlier place.

If you feel you don't have enough friends and your church is a "cold tomb" with "walls of cement," try to change those feelings—beginning with yours.

What Can Be Done About It?

Church leaders are trying to train people to make personal visits in order to reclaim dropouts. I am promoting the idea that in my church and yours we need never lose another member because we failed to be friendly. By being friendly, I am not talking about a nod or a handshake at the door. I do not have in mind the most hospitable smile and courteous greeting in the foyer by the best of greeters, as important as that is. Nor am I referring to a "friendship time" during the worship service when we stand and shake the hands of those around us. Such things are an important and excellent starting point, but they will not take the place of personal friendship!

I don't need someone to be friendly to me at church nearly as much as I need friendship outside the church service. It is during the week when I am struggling with everyday trials that I most need friendship. At such times I long for a friend whom I can call and ask to pray for me. I need friendship on Saturday night when I know that others are getting together. Nothing hurts more than to overhear a group talking about their plans for the evening and not be invited to join them! I desperately want and need their acceptance and their love—to feel that I belong to a group of friends who like and care about me.

The concept I am trying to get across to each churchgoing family is that we could transform the church—your church and mine—simply by changing how we relate to others. Sometimes we get so wrapped up in our cliques, or with family, that we have no time or need to include anyone else. But there are people out there who need *you—not someone else, but you.*

My Goal

My goal is to challenge you to begin practicing the delightful art of hospitality, to use your home for someone besides yourself and your own family, to experience what it means to "practice hospitality."

It is my prayer that the word "entertaining" will take on new meaning, one with spiritual significance and soul-winning potential. Whether you use the term "having company," "entertaining," "practice hospitality," or "throw a party," it matters little. The terminology is unimportant. What is important is that you feel the urgency to get involved in this indispensable ministry.

To learn the know-how of advance planning, menu preparation, gracious serving, table decorations, and the entertainment of guests—to become a master in this arena—is not an end in itself, as honorable a goal as that might be. Instead the real purpose is to use our homes to minister to those around us.

The practice of hospitality isn't an option for Christians, something we can elect to do if we feel like it. From a scriptural point of view, to neglect being hospitable is actual disobedience. Paul is forthright in his command to "Practice hospitality" (Rom. 12:13, NIV). Neither did Peter mince words when he said, "Offer hospitality to one another without grumbling" (1 Peter 4:9, NIV).

Many of us have resisted entertaining. We have taken the line of least resistance. If someone is coming over we stew, fret, and work ourselves into a frenzy, and we totally fall apart if anyone pops in on us unexpectedly. We tend to believe that our entire future hangs on how these people perceive the appearance of our homes, and how excellent the food was. We think of hospitality as a gift—a gift others have, *but not us!*

Thus we have an almost endless list of other excuses: my house isn't big enough; the children are too young; I'm not a good enough cook; my house is a mess; my husband or wife doesn't like to have company; my partner isn't a Christian and wouldn't approve; we need new furniture before I can entertain; we don't have enough money; I'm too busy; I don't know how to; and I'm too tired. All of these excuses rob us of a tremendous blessing, a blessing that God would pour out upon us as we entertain others and minister to their needs.

But there is no limit to what each one of us can do when we commit ourselves to ministering to others through hospitality. Regardless of your circumstance, it is possible for you to use your home as a place where others can find blessing, encouragement, and enjoyment.

In my travels over the past 20 plus years, I've been a guest in many homes. The vast majority of these homes have been beautifully decorated. The furniture has been carefully chosen and lends itself to an inviting and pleasant atmosphere. It is often obvious to me that the people of that home have put a tremendous amount of time, energy, and money into getting a certain "look."

I've met women who are excellent cooks, whom God has obviously blessed with superior talents in the kitchen. Some have table settings that are second to none. Their flowers or decorations are memorable and attractive. The talents and abilities that God has given them in decorating and turning their homes into places of beauty are outstanding. And they love to do it! To them this is not work. It is as natural as breathing.

To those talented homemakers I have a special appeal. God has given you your talents for a reason—to use them for Him. The ability to make your home beautiful, to decorate, to coordinate colors, to blend furniture styles and put it all together in a harmonious manner is not frivolous or wasted energy. To make a home comfortable for everyday family living as well as to say welcome to guests is truly a talent and gift from God.

Owning beautiful dishes, crystal, and silver is a blessing from God. To know how to create beautiful table settings and put it all together in an aesthetically inviting and attractive manner is a talent from God, as is the ability to take flowers and arrange them in a stunning manner. And to be a good, and possibly even a gourmet, cook is definitely a great gift from God.

Many people have such gifts and blessings, but either pay no attention to them or consider themselves as having done nothing significant for the Lord. They have never thought that every time they created a centerpiece, set the table, or cooked a meal for guests they were making a significant contribution to the work of God. "After all," they say, "I'm not giving Bible studies, witnessing, preaching, or teaching. I'm not doing anything for the Lord." Oh yes you are!

> *Kindness is more important than wisdom, and the recognition of this is the beginning of wisdom.*
>
> THEODORE ISAAC RUBIN

You need a totally new picture of the contribution you are making to the gospel commission to reach every nation, kindred, tongue, and people. While you may not be reaching around the globe, if you are opening your home to others, cooking, cleaning, and preparing for guests, you are fulfilling the gospel commission to "your world." As you do such things, you are making a significant and meaningful contribution to your friends and your church. And if you don't keep on doing what you are doing, the preacher, teacher, and healer won't have anyone left to preach to, teach, or heal!

All the time, effort, and money you have put into making your homes comfortable and beautiful places to live is not time and effort lost or wasted. All the cooking, vacuuming, dusting, cleaning, and decorating—all the money spent—has not been for nothing. If you are inviting others in to enjoy your home, it is money and time well spent. The church, the teacher, the evangelist, and healer need you to carry on. Without you to prepare attractive, comfortable homes our very church might fail. I applaud you.

Every time you feel exhausted from such efforts, remember to thank God that you had the strength to clean and prepare. And every time you plan a menu for guests and do the grocery shopping, thank God that He has provided you with the resources so you can entertain. Many might like to entertain with flair but lack the resources to do it. As you entertain, be thankful you have someone to encourage through your friendship. Many have no friends.

Hospitality is so much more than it appears on the surface. Through the gift of hospitality we can make friends and thus keep ourselves emotionally and socially healthy. We can also become a vital link in witnessing and proclaiming the gospel. But we can also, by extending hospitality to others, make the world a better place—a warmer and friendlier and infinitely more interesting place. Take your talents and carry on!

---

[1] Leo Schreven, "New Members and the Disappearing Act," *Adventist Review,* October 7, 1993, pp. 12-14.

[2] Peggy Harris, "Simply Restoring Simply," *Celebration,* December 1993, p. 10.

That special Book on the coffee table
of your home makes an excellent "silent witness."

4

HOSPITALITY: A POWERFUL WITNESS

ow can we best influence neighbors, coworkers, acquaintances, and possibly even nonattending members for the Lord? By ministering to their social needs—inviting people over for a meal or throwing a party. In other words, a powerful, almost untapped witnessing tool is **hospitality.** Almost everyone enjoys social occasions—a party atmosphere in which there is good food, good conversation, and a chance to meet other people. It is here that friendships begin.*

A practice from the world of real estate might teach us something. A realty firm in Salem, Oregon, assigns its agents a 500-family area. The agent must contact each family once a month for a year via phone, letter, or a personal visit. Research indicates that it takes at least six contacts for people to remember who the agent is and whom he or she represents. The real estate company encourages its agents to build relationships only, not to try to get in the home, gain a listing, or make a sale. Since everyone else is also trying to get in the door, such an approach is good psychology at this point. Getting acquainted is the main goal at first. But research shows that when an agent follows this pattern for one and a half years, he or she will get 80 percent of the listings in the area.

Several real estate agents in our neighborhood must employ this principle. I do not recall with what regularity they contact us, but we receive notices about what homes in our neighborhood are for sale and have been sold by a certain agent. Recently someone left a business card at our front door. The card had a picture and a message from the agent who sold us our home 18 years ago! I imagine that when and if we ever decide to sell, we would list with her. Although we aren't exactly "friends," she's there, accessible, and knows our neighborhood. I trust her.

Is there a principle here that real estate agents understand and operate by that we may have overlooked? First, people do not like "strangers" knocking on their doors, let alone trying to get into their homes. This is especially true now with the crime wave currently sweeping America. Where a salesperson does gain entry to a home, he or she encounters a strong determination not to be "taken in" by some phony sales pitch for commercial goods the residents have never heard of. However, if a friend comes over with the same product and gives a glowing testimonial about its effectiveness, an individual is much more likely to buy. A satisfied customer is a most effective salesperson.

> *A new friend is like new wine; when it has aged you will drink it with pleasure.*
> ECCLESIASTES 9:10

Second, people are more likely to do business with friends and acquaintances rather than with strangers. Third, it takes time to build the right climate. Fourth, when witnessing in this manner, you want to make haste slowly.

Whether you live in a housing development, in a rural area, or in an apartment complex, you are surrounded by potential members, persons not yet ready for formal Bible studies, but who would respond to a gesture of friendship or hospitality. Obviously you cannot adopt a 500-family section as real estate agents do in Salem, but you can select a co-worker or three or four families and begin to work through them to see who might be the most responsive. Block parties, neighborhood watch programs, Christmas open houses, neighborhood drop-ins, plus other casual social activities provide excellent ways to start in mixing hospitality with evangelism.

Get Acquainted

Next you will need to get acquainted with these three or four families. Here is where you will have to persevere in prayer as you ask God to help you know how to approach your neighbors so you can get acquainted. Carefully learn their names and how to pronounce them correctly. Be friendly each opportunity you have to be around the people. Smile and be happy. A happy, committed Christian is a living testimony. Your neighbors may even begin asking questions about the source of your happiness. Think of the negative impact you might make on other families by a silent, unsmiling, unapproachable manner! But through a winning smile and pleasant attitude you can make an excellent first impression.

Next . . . Talk to These People

In order to build any kind of friendship you've got to talk to people. Many get really tongue-tied when attempting to speak with others "not of their own brand." But if you really take care to learn the art of conversing, you won't be so frightened of it. Why? Because you will actually say less than the other person. A good conversationalist is better at asking insightful questions and listening than at talking.

Have at your fingertips some subjects of a general nature that you can introduce—their profession or career, their children's school and accomplishments, sports, hobbies, gardening, vacations, current news makers, home improvement projects, books and films. If the person is a neighbor, look for a boat, car, pet, garden, or something else that will allow you to connect further. "I'm a quilter too. I need some help with a border I'm working on. Please come in and give me some advice." Share gardening tips or vegetables from your garden, or pitch in and help with home repairs. Now you are building a natural, comfortable bridge to invite him or her into your home.

Invite Them Into Your Home

Some of you are probably saying at this point, "I can't do that!" And if you are, you're probably right. You never will. But God says you can. He says, "Practice hospitality." While it was a special directive to elders and church leaders, you can still handle it because He also says you can do all things through Him (Phil 4:13). Now, which will you choose to believe? What God tells you or the negative messages you are feeding yourself? If you say you can't do it, you are actually saying you will not do it. But if you say that you can do it, you certainly will.

Remember also the general pattern for evangelism. Witnessing begins with friendship. Unless you are in public evangelism, it is very difficult to proclaim the gospel to someone you do not know. Even then the evangelist will have greater successes with those with whom he has established personal relationships.

By inviting someone to your home, you start the process for cultivating a friendship. And once you have established a friendship, you will become aware of your friend's needs. Then you can begin responding with spiritual answers to both what the person feels he or she needs and what the person really needs. Your friend now trusts you and sees evidence of the gospel in your life. If you attempt to introduce topics or give answers before you know the person's needs, you will be premature and often misjudge or mishandle the situation.

Your goal so far has been to advance your acquaintance, and in the case of neighbors, your back-fence relationship toward a more significant friendship. A meal around a table is one of the best ways of bonding this new relationship. It seems to be easier if there is an occasion or a reason for having them over. Think of sharing a new recipe, celebrating a birthday, enjoying homemade ice cream, or watching videos of a recent vacation (not six hours of them, however!).

A big difference exists between entertaining your church friends, who probably all share your spiritual values, and using the gift of hospitality as a witnessing tool. You can mix the two, but you must do it judiciously. We all know people like overzealous Aunt Matilda and super saint Brother Benjamin who try to turn every conversation into an eschatological study of the 10 horns of the beast of Daniel 7. What started out as a friendly opportunity to mix church friends socially with those of differing or no faith turns into a discussion in which well-intentioned members hammered home their favorite hobbyhorse.

A friend is someone who knows your song, and sings it to you when you forget it.

But how freeing and refreshing it can be to bring people of differing religious backgrounds together for a social occasion only and then leave the results to God Himself. If we fully trust the convicting power of the Holy Spirit, our strategy can be low-key and pleasant, but very successful over time.

Create a Comfortable Atmosphere

The first thing that you must do is to create an atmosphere in your home in which the nonmember feels "at home." Often church members are insensitive to the group dynamics of such an occasion. The church friends you have invited to your social event need to understand in advance your purpose for extending hospitality to the nonmember, or they may quickly drive him or her away. Nonmembers will feel comfortable in the mixed group only when they sense that others accept and like them. For an evening of such entertaining, it might be good to have each church couple bring their own nonmember guest. That way you can be more sure of their sensitivity and attitudes of acceptance.

For such entertaining, as host or hostess you need to think through and lay down some ground rules that you and your other church friends agree upon and understand. The first purpose of the get-together is to mix church friends with people who are not members. The second is that you must make the nonmembers feel welcome. Third, topics for discussion that come up around the table and beyond must be appropriate for and include nonmembers. In other words, it is not the time for anyone to give a Bible study, ride a favorite biblical hobbyhorse, put down or make derogatory remarks about other denominations, or try to straighten out any religious views expressed.

Friendly, cheerful conversation of both a personal and general nature should dominate the scene. During such general conversation many nuggets of truth-filled lives will shine forth to the nonmember completely unknown to you. The Holy Spirit knows and understands your purpose in entertaining, and will take your words and lay them upon the hearts of all those present, leaving sparks of truth, joy, and friendship that can and will be an influence for good later on. You cannot let yourself get impatient with your efforts at this point, but must look only at the long term results and trust the Holy Spirit to bless the seeds you are planting through the hospitality you have extended.

One thing that you must avoid at all cost is the "holy huddle"—any group or clique from the church chatting together (especially in "holy conversation") and thus excluding in both their huddle and their talk nonmember guests. I've seen the saints do this to newcomers. And forgive my bluntness at this point (along with what might be termed a sexist remark), but women are especially cruel to each other. If a woman has a friend or group of friends she feels safe with at a social occasion, she will only rarely leave the security of the group to welcome or get to know a newcomer. And should the newcomer be dressed inappropriately or in opposition to the "in-group's" standard or criteria, few at the event will even welcome her, let alone try to become her friend. Christian maturity demands that we move beyond our comfortable cocoons of safety.

Keep It Simple

A good rule of thumb if you are having someone over for the first time is to **keep it simple.** A formal five-course sit-down dinner with crystal, china, and sterling silver might overwhelm many people. A formal table setting sets the stage for a more formal affair. Good friends can relax in a formal atmosphere, but here we are still trying to get acquainted. Patio dining or an outdoor picnic might make new guests feel more at home the first time. An elaborate meal and table setting may be especially intimidating if a woman guest feels she could never match it. You'll likely discourage her and never get an invitation to her home. The loss here is not a meal or a payback, but another opportunity to build the friendship. You can still serve the meal in a creative manner. It can and should be attractively done—just not overdone.

A potluck dinner invitation is a great way to get people together in an informal manner. It means less work for the host, and people feel more a part of the group if they have contributed something to the meal, especially if it gets rave reviews. Everyone seems to enjoy a meal of good food and fellowship—church member or not. Some of God's most significant work can take place around a table filled with nutritious food and warm friendship.

Once you get your nonmember guests to your table, don't feel you have to say "something spiritual" in order to make the event successful or to accomplish your goal! Many people feel they have failed to witness properly if they haven't said something to influence the person for truth. This is where patience and discerning the leading of the Holy Spirit come in. One Christian couple entertained nonmember friends around their table about 30 times in three years before spiritual topics could be discussed. But the payoff for their patience came eventually when the time was right. This couple became tremendous workers for the Lord.

As the group begins to bond and you observe personalities beginning to click as conversations take off in many different directions, again resist the temptation to start a Bible study or dump a load of spiritual talk on your captive audience. Leave the converting entirely to the Holy Spirit, while you focus on seeing that your guests have fun and enjoy warm fellowship. Certainly you want to be sensitive to the leading of the Holy Spirit, but you also must use common sense. For the time being, the informal, secular conversation going on around the table is performing a most valuable function. It is breaking barriers down. While people are testing each other's personal reactions to the topics entering the discussion, they are also forming bonds with each other.

Ask the Holy Spirit's guidance in initiating a spiritual topic. Better yet, ask the Holy Spirit to have your guest ask questions when the time is right. What is important over the meal is that no one gets the feeling that he or she is an "outsider" looking in on the "inner circle." Each guest needs to feel a level of comfort as early as possible at the occasion, a sense of both belonging to the group and being liked by others.

If you feel socially inept and awkward, especially around unbelieving or unchurched friends, work with someone from your church who is a good conversationalist and has a profound gift for hospitality. Have this person or family join you and your nonchurch member friends for a meal. Blend your church friend's gift for hospitality with your own concern for your new nonmember friends, and you'll have a winning combination. See if your socially adept church friends wouldn't be excited to use their social skills to assist you in bonding the relationship.

Let There Be Laughter
Use all the humor you possibly can during the occasion without

being ridiculous. Let the laughter flow. Encourage it. All of us live such high-stress lives that we need to be able to let loose with some good laughs. It's good for the body, mind, and spirit, and encourages better mental, physical, and spiritual health. Your new non-member guests need to discover that committed Christians can have a good time—even without alcohol to boost the mood level.

Personal stories about yourself can bring laughter when used appropriately. Instead of telling only about your successes, relate a captivating story about a failure. Failure stories can be funny and yet offer valuable lessons about life, and your belief system can shine through them. Whatever you do, relax. This is your party. These are your guests. Enjoy them and the occasion.

Prayer becomes a very important part of hospitality evangelism. You will want to pray for the leading of the Holy Spirit in planning the event. The guest list needs special prayer and guidance. Good preplanning along with prayer over all your preparation will give you greater

> *One can never speak enough of the virtues and power of shared laughter.*
> FRANCOISE SAGAN

confidence as you begin to rely more on the Holy Spirit as you reach out to others in this type of entertaining. Prayer for the event and those attending as well as follow-up prayers for your guests will avail much. As you continuously practice your new skills in hospitality and undergird them with prayer, you will feel more confident and accumulate unnumbered successes.

But please don't attempt to count your successes only in terms of how many people begin attending church, begin Bible studies, or are baptized! This is a very narrow, shallow interpretation of what hospitality offers. We more often number successes in intangibles—encouragement for the discouraged, friendship for the lonely, a good laugh for the disheartened, a chance to glimpse Christ through you.

Make your home an open circle of hospitality whether or not you ever see anyone baptized. If nonmembers become friends, you will have more opportunities to influence them for Christ. And that's what hospitality evangelism is all about. Living open, beautiful lives so that through our circle of relationships others can see Christ's beauty working in us.

Handling Difficult Situations Graciously

It just might be that in reaching out to people of differing or no faith you might encounter some difficult situations. Should your guests, in a gesture of friendship, bring to your home a bottle of alcohol, you must be prepared to handle it graciously and wisely. Bringing a bottle of alcohol is a common practice among secular people and a gesture of friendship. It is hardly the time for a lecture on the evils of liquor. A self-righteous attitude is neither appropriate nor biblical.

Think through your options. If your conscience does not allow you, even under the circumstances, to accept what someone has brought you as a gift, graciously decline and return it to them. Or you may accept it and later dispose of it.

Should any of your guests ask to smoke, graciously tell them that because of health reasons you'd prefer they step outside. Don't encourage someone to smoke by having an ashtray outside, however.

Some question whether we should say a blessing for the meal in front of such guests. Yes, by all means! This is your home, and saying a blessing is a natural part of your family life. The prayer should be very much like always—no let's-try-to-slip-in-a-subtle-Bible-study-here business. It could be very effective to thank God for each guest by name. At a restaurant it might be better to have silent prayer, as this may be too embarrassing for your guests to handle in public.

Make Holidays Count

Holidays are some of the best occasions to invite nonmembers to our homes. Both Christmas and Thanksgiving provide a natural platform with spiritual undertones. Consider a Christmas open house, not for people at church who are already your friends, but for those on your block or at your office. Sing carols together. Have each guest share a moment from a holiday past. There is no need for a formal Bible study or witness program here. Your home is your witness. You are witnessing through the gift of hospitality. People are often more open to spiritual matters during holidays. Just provide the opportunity and let God work on their hearts. Use Christian decorations and Christmas cards and really play down Santa on the tree.

Minister to the Hurting

When people are hurting, they need help and are most responsive and thankful for help from others. Sickness, death of a family member, marital stress, loss of a job or business, financial reversals, or a major problem with a teenager all provide opportunities for the Christian to serve and care for others. One author says, "People don't care how much or what you know until they know how much you care!" A helping hand, a listening ear, some food brought to their home, an invitation for a meal—all give validity to your beliefs. You can shop for these people, run errands, drive, care for children, do laundry—all these are faith-in-action steps.

When conversing with hurting people, be real. Let them know that you understand their hurt and pain. Perhaps God has prepared you through the loss of a loved one. Caution: do not take over the conversation and do all the talking. It is a gross error some make when ministering to others. The hurting person needs a listening ear, not a talking mouth—a listener who will empathize and *just be there,* often in comfortable silence.

When people are hurting, it is an excellent time to give them an article or book to read, something that speaks to their present heartfelt need and points them to Christ as the supreme problem solver. If they are struggling with personal family problems, you might want to give them such books as *Compleat Marriage, To Have and to Hold, Compleat Parent, Train Up a Child, From This Day Forward,* or *How to Talk So Your Mate Will Listen,* depending on the nature of the stress.

Each of us needs to have a supply of Christian resources at our fingertips to lend or give out when appropriate. My sister, Ginger Snarr, has really taught me a few things here. She purchases my book *From This Day Forward: Blueprint for Family Happiness* by the hundreds and gives them out wherever she goes, to people I'd never think of handing them to. She travels outside the United States with me when Harry isn't available, and always has 10 or more tucked in her carry-on luggage. Some of the more interesting people she's shared books with have been a medical missionary doctor on his way to the Bahamas to do a month of relief work in a Catholic hospital; Tom Pukstys, the 1989 Olympic javelin champion; flight attendants; and managers of hotels that we have stayed at. I believe God frequently puts people in our path, people who need to be ministered to.

> *Put your heart, mind, intellect, and soul even to your smallest acts. This is the secret of success.*

A good book on the coffee table of your home makes an excellent "silent witness." Books that are need-centered as opposed to doctrinal ones are more appropriate for the unchurched. What you are looking for here is a book with such appeal that it draws people to pick it up, thumb through it, and ask questions. This could lead to a good conversation on some topic with great spiritual overtones. Let your nonmember guests lead with the questions. Be casual and alert to unspoken questions. What is really being asked? Is there a deeper or underlying problem they are struggling with?

Offer to lend the book. A loaned book is frequently more effective than a gift book. A loaned book must be returned, placing responsibility on the other person to actually read it, return it, and to say something when bringing it back. If you do a lot of this type of witnessing and want your books back, you'd better keep track of where they go, however.

Social relationships are the key to influencing people for Christ. And those who respond to you socially will be your best candidates. As you become convinced of the possibilities offered through hospitality evangelism and begin opening your home for more and more social occasions to both members and nonmembers, always remember that some will respond and some won't. Don't become discouraged over those who do not. Some responded to Christ's personal invitation to follow Him and some didn't. We are simply to be about the King's business. Let the Holy Spirit do His job. Our responsibility is to reflect Jesus and introduce Him and encourage others.

---

*Material in this chapter is adapted from Joseph Aldrich, *Lifestyle Evangelism* (Portland, Oreg.: Multnomah Press, 1981).

*Something fun our women's ministry group
just did was to have an indoor February beach party.*

5

THE HOSPITALITY GAME PLAN

ave you ever heard anyone say something like "Let Rob and Shari do it. They give great parties. There's nothing to it for them"? Please don't believe that it's easy for such people, however. Rob and Shari have worked hard to make it look effortless. But behind the scenes a lot has been going on in order to give that appearance. Both have prepared thoroughly before the event.

You too can achieve that effortless look when you have made proper planning and preparation in advance. Entertaining is an art—the art of bringing people together for an enjoyable time. And just as is the case with other artists, you will learn by doing. The more you entertain, the easier it becomes as you discover what does and doesn't work for you. Soon you will develop your own personal style.

Almost anyone can cook a meal and have a group over to eat it. But the most successful entertaining contains three ingredients: planning, organization, and creativity. What makes the difference between just another gathering of people and a memorable occasion is a sincere desire to extend hospitality to others.

Organization is the key to hosting an event that runs smoothly whether it is a cozy dinner for four or a big bash for 40. The host that looks relaxed at any party is one who takes care of all details long before the guests arrive. Good food and attractive decorations are a vital part of entertaining, but a relaxed and confident host is even more important.

Entertaining should not be a dreaded burden. Rather, it should provide you with pleasure and satisfaction. Hopefully the information in this chapter will allow you to plan effectively as well as inspire you to entertain often.*

Decide the Type of Event

First determine what kind of event you would like to have. A formal dinner party requires a different time, menu, and planning than a backyard picnic. In addition, both call for different locations and decorations. You might also have a totally different guest list, since one is quite casual and the other more formal. The type of event will determine the time, date, guest list, menu, and many other things.

Think through what kind of event suits your reason for entertaining. Are you hosting a seasonal party for close friends that includes seasonal decorations, menus, games, and a festive atmosphere? Or is your purpose to gather neighbors with a let's-get-acquainted theme? The latter event might not include a whole menu, but rather only dessert. Decide early on the nature of the event you are hosting, as this affects most other decisions.

Deciding the type of event can be either the most difficult or the most fun choice, depending on your personality. Some of you may wish to stay with the tried-and-true methods of entertaining—what is fully accepted in your crowd and what you are comfortable with. You are not very adventuresome and don't wish to go out on a limb and take chances with some new type of entertaining that makes you uncomfortable.

Others of you are more creative and are looking for some new ideas to make the old group come alive. You will enjoy all the creative ideas suggested in the book for giving tables, centerpieces, food, and people all a "new look."

Choose the Location

The next decision involves *where* you will entertain your guests. Some of you may say, "In the dining room, of course!" However, you don't have to confine entertaining to one room. Some entertaining lends itself nicely to being spread throughout the house. You can set tables up in the living room, for example. Or you can entertain on the patio, by the pool, on the lawn, in a park, at the beach, or by a mountain stream. When planning an outdoor location, always have a backup indoor site just in case it rains.

Prepare a Guest List

When you entertain, you can play it safe and invite the same old group—people who already know and like one another. But this can get as dull as serving the same menu every time. Or you can decide to invite a new face every time you entertain. It is my belief that every in crowd needs a new face once in a while. It might be someone new from church, the accoun-

A friend is a present you give yourself.
ROBERT LOUIS STEVENSON

tant from your office, or a neighbor. This will give the same old group some new things to talk about and provide better entertainment for all.

If your real purpose is to get to know someone new, think through the categories of people to invite. They include married couples with children, married couples without children, single adults, the elderly, teenagers and college students, secular friends, neighbors, work associates, and people met through business and social contacts.

The tendency when making up a guest list is to stick with friends—those we know and like. We want to be with them because we have much in common to discuss with them. It's easier to pick such people because you don't have to fuss, worry, or strain to make conversation. You know what to expect before they arrive.

But if we are going to use hospitality in the way God intended, we must move beyond our "safe cliques," our known circle of friends. I'm not suggesting you never see them again. But I do urge you to include someone else with your friends. There are many great people out there that we never get to know because we never give them an opportunity to meet us. We can reach out to those who are lonely, hurting, or discouraged, ones who need a friend to listen and care, people who would love to get to know us. *Every time you entertain, include someone outside your circle of friends.*

This concept is deeply biblical. "Then Jesus said to his host, 'When you give a luncheon or dinner, do not invite your friends, your brothers or relatives, or your rich neighbors; if you do, they may invite you back and so you will be repaid. But when you give a banquet, invite the poor, the crippled, the lame, the blind, and you will be blessed. Although they cannot repay you, you will be repaid at the resurrection of the righteous" (Luke 14:12-14, NIV).

Entertaining such people puts no great burden on us. They do not demand an elaborate meal, nor do you need to try to impress them with fancy dishes, gorgeous centerpieces, new furniture, a spacious home, or an elaborate meal. Instead they will simply appreciate a warm welcome and any food you have prepared. Your friendship, and the opportunity to be with you, will be a glimpse of heaven to them.

Not long ago I invited six older women for dinner after church. None had ever been to my home before, and they did not contribute to the meal. I didn't want them to. It was something I wanted to do for them. Invitations to dinner are probably few and far between for these women, all widows. Two were slightly crippled, and one couldn't hear well. But that was all right with me. I wanted to do something for others with no thought of a pay back. The women couldn't have done so even if they had wanted to. Their entertaining days had long passed. But even yet these ladies extend their thin, wrinkled hands and warm smiles to me. I am the one who was blessed from the experience.

When drawing up the guest list, include people from varying backgrounds. For example, if you are a teacher and want to entertain other teachers, the event could quickly deteriorate into shoptalk. Some of this is OK, but when this dominates the conversation, it can get boring to those not part of the teaching profession.

Think twice before you speak, especially if you intend to say what you think.

It is also a great idea to mix generations—the old with the young and married couples with singles. Seat a teenage niece next to the oldest guest rather than all youngsters at one end of the table and the older ones at the other end. There is a magic quality that comes from mixing generations. Singles also need a place around our tables. One of their greatest needs is to be included in family get-togethers. The event at which guests may linger the longest is one in which there has been an effective mix of generations and other categories of people.

How Many Should Be Invited?

Decide the number of people you can handle. Sometimes bigger is better. In a larger group people mix and converse easier. More people make more noise, and it sounds like everyone is talking and laughing at the same time. As a result, it appears safer and more relaxing. Four people don't make much noise. Each person then has to work harder in order for the conversation to flow. Everyone bears more responsibility to participate. Some enjoy this but others don't, since it tends to make them self-conscious around those they do not know well.

The size of your table, the flow of space between rooms, your budget, and your method of serving will also determine the number of people you invite. A smaller home or apartment generally means a smaller number of guests. You can get around this by setting up additional tables or serving buffet-style, however.

Be realistic about how many people you can entertain at one time comfortably in your home. You may want to have a certain group at once and get it over with, but that isn't always possible. It may be necessary to have two separate parties, which, with good planning, could be held on consecutive days. I have done this at Christmas and on other occasions when I wanted to use the same decorations. It works wonderfully well, and you have a major cleanup only one time, so there are advantages.

Doesn't Bigger Cost More?

Sometimes, but it doesn't have to. There are ways of getting around the heavy expenses involved. One approach is to entertain with another couple. I've done this countless times. It seems I always have a friend or two who also feel the crunch when it comes to having others over. But sharing the responsibility and dividing the meal make it all possible. We each invite someone of our choice and share in some great entertaining ventures together.

The first time I invite people to my home I rarely ask or permit them to contribute to a meal. But after that, especially if they offer, I will gladly accept help in putting the menu together. Sharing the cost and the work makes it easier for all involved. And it is the only way to handle a large group. On a written invitation specify what you would like to have them bring. When inviting people in person, you can wait to see if they volunteer, or simply say, "A few of us are getting together for dinner after church. We are all sharing in preparing the meal. Would you like to join us?" This lets them know up front that the invitation includes participation in meal preparation.

Or you can invite people over for dessert only. Far too often food becomes the focal point of entertaining. While food is important, true hospitality goes beyond just feeding people. Although food helps us achieve our goal of offering encouragement and friendship, we must keep even this in perspective. In our society, however, to invite people over and not feed them is almost crass. It is much easier to talk and get acquainted around a table with a meal. Food helps us attain this goal, and it is an important one.

Sharing the cost of the meal and the workload involved in entertaining means less work for the host, but it also means something for guests—they will be more committed and interested in making a success of the event, since they have a stake in it too.

Plan the Menu

The perfect guest menu is a delicate balancing act between flavors, textures, and colors without taxing your budget or workload. You can cut expensive dishes into smaller portions and balance them with elaborate platters of vegetables. Menus should also blend textures, flavors, and colors. Something crunchy should follow something creamy smooth. In your mind first serve up the entire menu on the plate and make sure the colors are varied and interesting.

Let the season be your guide. For example, serve asparagus, strawberries, and tomatoes when in season and most economical. Each season has its particular pleasures, and they are worth exploiting.

Select a menu that fits your schedule. If you have little time on the day of the event to prepare, follow a menu that you can prepare in stages beforehand. Otherwise, it is a good idea to plan dishes that you can do at the last minute as guests arrive.

Choose a menu appropriate for the number of guests you are serving. If you are planning a chili feed for young marrieds, do you have a pot that will hold chili for a possible 30? Do you have ample oven, refrigerator, and burner space for the menu and number of people you have invited?

If you asked me what I think is the most important prerequisite for planning a successful party, I would say: "Keep it simple!"

I love to entertain, but I simply will not be in the kitchen working while my guests are in the living room having fun. Over the years I have developed numerous recipes that I can pull from the oven or refrigerator and have table ready in minutes. This takes careful planning in advance of the arrival of my guests.

The week before the event I write out the full menu, everything to be served right down to relishes and butter. Next I check the ingredients of each recipe against my existing supplies. I make a list of what I need and purchase it during my regular grocery shopping on Wednesday.

Method of Serving

Determining how you serve a meal can be as important as the menu itself. Choose a method that you enjoy and is comfortable for you. You might select a sit-down meal in the dining room or you might prefer a serve-yourself buffet at which people will gather on the patio, by the fireplace, under a backyard tree, or on the bank of a nearby stream. A survey of your home and yard may reveal ideas that you've never thought of before—porches, cozy nooks, or even cleared-out garages or attics.

In character,
in manner, in style,
in all things,
the supreme excellence
is simplicity.
LONGFELLOW

Be inventive. Something fun our women's ministry group just did was to have an indoor February beach party. Women came dressed in beach clothing and sat in beach chairs and on beach towels before a roaring fire in the fireplace. The meal was served buffet-style from a sandy setting of shells and pails and shovels on the dining table.

Before the event, mentally serve everyone according to your plan. Where will you put the buffet table or extra dining table or serving cart? For larger parties, you can rearrange the furniture. During the indoor beach party I mentioned earlier, all my country-style furnishings went onto the patio to give more space. Where will food be set? Will you have a punch bowl and where will it go? At a sit-down meal you want to make guests feel comfortable, not crowded. For a true buffet you'll want to create reasons for people to circulate after eating.

Table Settings

Plan the table settings two weeks in advance in order to give yourself time to develop ideas and gather and purchase all supplies. Wash linens and purchase candles. When planning more than one table, visualize the look desired for each table. Remember that tables do not have to match or be identical. Each table can have a different appearance, but the effect achieved should complement or be harmonious with the others.

The centerpiece can be as simple as a fruit bowl or as elaborate as a winter wonderland ice sculpture. Whatever you choose, it should not obstruct the view of diners across the table, although buffet centerpieces can and should be tall. Flowers from your yard, the street corner, or the local supermarket are always appropriate. One of my favorite centerpieces is white Shasta daisies placed in a clear glass pitcher—simple yet perky and refreshing. Whereas flowers are not the only suitable centerpiece, fresh flowers do lend a specialness to the occasion.

Plan Activities and Entertainment*

You need to carefully plan and think through what to do after a meal. Some people like to sit and visit, others enjoy board games or some other activity. Getting people you do not know well involved in activities that will please everyone can be tricky. For this reason I prefer entertaining around a theme in which the activity is "built-in." Examples might be a spa or pool party, an "election party," in which the group follows the election results, an old-fashioned Christmas party, a Super Bowl party, or a pancake breakfast in the mountains followed by a hike and a game of horseshoes.

But good conversation is one of the nicest things that can happen after a meal. Nothing can replace it, especially if your goal is to get to know your guests better and establish a friendship.

In this case, the conversation may continue around the table, or you may ask people to join you in the living room, in the family room, on the patio, or wherever. Some may enjoy a hot or cold drink at this time. But you do not have to spend every minute caring for all their needs because it is time for you to enjoy your guests. This should be the most enjoyable portion of the occasion for you.

If you try to move people to another area, an interesting dynamic takes over. The women immediately jump up to help with the dishes and the men drift to another room. Now the men talk "men talk" and the women "women talk." Probably the sexes will cease to mix. Some of this is all right. Women need "women talk," but it can get boring and tedious.

It is perfectly all right for the host to remain at the table with her guests as long as she likes, remembering that the minute she gets up to clear the table, it will break the conversational flow. On one occasion after church we entertained the pastor and his wife. We had an excellent mix of people and much stimulating conversation. At 4:30 we were still seated around the table when the pastor said, "This is the first time I've ever been allowed to stay at the table and just talk. Everyone always wants to move into the living room and 'get comfortable.' I really appreciate being able to stay at the table and talk with all these great people."

The best guide to conversation is to ask questions.

There are only a few social occasions on which you should turn the television on: Election Day, a State of the Union address, a Tournament of Roses Parade, a Super Bowl, or some other momentous event. Outside of such occasions, however, television will only intrude when you are trying to build bridges between guests.

Gently discourage those who try to catch a basketball game or keep up with some regular show. One could call such guests little more than TV addicts. They in fact are saying to the hosts that they find the company so boring that they must substitute their favorite program for their hosts' presence.

What happens after the meal is every bit as important as what takes place during it as you attempt to build bridges between people. Use the occasion to its full potential.

Rehearse the Event in Your Mind

In advance of the event, picture every detail of it in your mind. Visualize how your home will look with the lighting adjusted and how guests will sit in the living room. Imagine how you will greet each person at the door, what will be said, and what you can do to make people comfortable at that point. What special touches might you add to make it more special and comfortable?

In your mind's eye, move to the dining area. Picture the table with the centerpiece in place and the table set. Think through where each guest should sit and what conversation might take place around the table. Imagine how you want the food to look and taste and how it will be served. Visualize also what you expect to have happen following the meal.

Once you have thoroughly rehearsed the event in your mind, you can be more confident and relaxed. As long as you are uptight about all the preparations you are not free to minister to the needs of your guests in the way you should. By thinking through every detail, you gain confidence. A more confident you means a more relaxed host.

If your guests sense that you are frazzled, rushed, or anxious, they will not be able to relax. It is imperative, then, that you get your mind off yourself and the individual tasks that need to be done. Only then will you really be able to meet their needs fully.

Entertaining Alone

Unfortunately many singles still think that they need a partner to entertain, and thus miss opportunities to offer hospitality as a result. Their excuses are many: "I don't know how to cook anymore. I eat out all the time . . . I will entertain again when I get married . . . I can't entertain, as my place is too small . . . My entertaining days are over since my husband died. I don't see any of my former friends."

The purpose of entertaining is to extend hospitality and encouragement to others. This puts the single person in a tremendous position to share such things with persons the married couple may not even be aware of. And you do not have to be married, prepare an elaborate meal, or have a large home in order to accomplish both goals. You can offer hospitality and encouragement as easily in a one-room apartment as in a mansion.

True creativeness is finding new possibilities in old situations.

Nor do you have to invite a large crowd. Some of the best social occasions occur when only one or two guests are present. Look for opportunities—a former classmate who has come to town, your son's roommate from college, a colleague from work whom you'd like to get to know, a single person from church who you know is hurting. What better way to minister to people than at your home, as humble or small as it may be?

Harry and I were guests at the apartment of a 34-year-old single who was the coordinator for a Compleat Marriage Seminar we were teaching on the coast of California. I was startled when we received an invitation for dinner at his home rather than the pastor's. Yet it was a delightful experience. And he handled it with class— spaghetti, tossed salad, an excellent dressing he called his "specialty," garlic bread, and ice cream for dessert. A simple menu, but very much appreciated because of the friendship extended. His warm outgoing personality combined with his lovingly prepared meal remains in my memory as an outstanding example of what a single person—even a single man—can do to entertain.

A separate dining area is an asset but not a necessity. It does make the perfect setting for a seated dinner or buffet. But many newer apartments do not have a formal dining area. In such cases use the kitchen area. It is less formal, but you can dress it up by making it as elegant as you like. If you don't have a dining area, you can convert a coffee table, low chest, desktop, or modular wall system. Use what space you have.

You may be terrified of trying to get all the food ready at once by yourself. Planning and cooking ahead will simplify matters. But there are also alternatives if you can't handle it alone. Check out a local delicatessen or bakery for a special cheese-and-spinach quiche or a homemade dessert. Get something new and different that will surprise and delight your guests. It is also perfectly acceptable to order in Chinese food from a local restaurant. Or you may ask each guest to bring one item that completes your menu.

When entertaining alone, the important point to remember is that you are offering hospitality and encouragement, not trying to put on the dinner party of the century. Keep things simple, plan ahead, and accept a little help from your friends. Then your parties will be events that anyone will enjoy.

Whether you are an experienced host or a determined and dedicated beginner, you must carefully follow the game plan for successful entertaining. Your warm and gracious welcome, skilled preparations, and competence in stimulating the flow of conversation mean more than honoring traditional social rules. The warmth you project as host gives each guest a comfort zone, a feeling of being pampered and very special.

Lest you think all my entertaining is a smash hit, don't you believe it!

My mother has a home in southern California, and I frequently entertain family and friends when visiting her. Entertaining can get a bit tricky in someone else's home. One time I baked the casserole before leaving for church so that it only needed warming when I returned. From another room I heard my mother call, "Leave it in the oven and prop the door open." I questioned this but did as instructed. When I returned home after church I got a whiff of something burning. The casserole was a charcoal crisp. It was then that my mother explained in detail that she thought I knew to turn the oven off and that the pilot light would continue to keep it warm. Needless to say, we shifted to plan B—good old spaghetti.

Even I make mistakes when entertaining, but you know what? Everyone who has done so has escaped the obituary column—including me. So if you host an event or two where something goes wrong or is a complete flop, at least you're trying! Lift your head, kick up your heels, and go for it again. A mistake or two doesn't have to crush you unless you allow it to.

---

*Ideas in this chapter are adapted from Marlene D. Le Fever, *Creative Hospitality* (Wheaton, Ill.: Tyndale House Publishers, 1980); *Entertaining for all Seasons* (Menlo Park, Calif.: Lane Publishing Co., 1984).

Besides Le Fever, two other excellent resources for types of entertainment are Maralys Wills, *Fun Games for Great Parties* (Los Angeles: Price, Stern, Sloan) and Karol Ladd, *Parties With a Purpose* (Nashville: Thomas Nelson).

Le Fever's book is an out-of-the-ordinary guide to purposeful parties to get people ministering and to reach out to newcomers. It has complete party plans from invitations, name tags, and decorations to menus, projects, and follow-up. Wills has hundreds of exciting new games for all kinds of parties. And Ladd has ideas for creating memorable children's parties. Every party centers around a theme, with related games, crafts, party favors, and a Bible story. Even the suggested food relates to the theme.

*There can be true beauty in simplicity,
and there is a real art to learning how to serve a simple meal in an elegant style.*

HOSPITALITY PLUS

he role of host is neither trivial nor frivolous, since it is vital to the social functioning of the home, the church, and society in general. Here are a few tips that will help you sparkle with "hospitality plus." [1]

Review Guests' Names in Advance

About a week before you entertain, make up two copies of the guest list. Put one in the kitchen window so you can review the names of everyone invited. Hopefully you have invited someone not part of "your group," making this step especially necessary. Put the other list on the dresser for your partner to review. Both of you can then get all names clearly in mind before the event. Master any difficult pronunciations. Repeat them aloud until they roll off your tongue easily.

Guest of Honor Know-how

Strict rules of etiquette suggest that you should seat a female guest of honor to the right of the male host and a male guest of honor to the right of the female host. But I'm happy to get any seat at all. If there is to be a guest of honor who will not know all the other guests, provide the individual a list of the other names ahead of time. That has been a lifesaver for me. Sometimes I am invited to a meal or a dinner with committees who want me to teach a seminar. Some seminar coordinators provide me with a list of the names of those present and their positions on the committee. This has been a tremendous help in remembering names and initiating conversation.

Written Invitations

Written invitations are only necessary for more formal occasions nowadays. When possible, tie the invitation to the theme of your event. For example, I used invitations for a Christmas party computer printed on green paper and cut out in the shape of a Christmas tree. Dots of sparkle puff paint provided the finishing touch. With your invitation also include a map with directions to your home. It's a good idea to carry this map with you at all times. Then after church you can invite guests impromptu and help them locate your home more easily.

No Rule for success will work if you don't.

Should you include an RSVP on an invitation, you will usually find it necessary to check back with those invited. People know what RSVP means, but lead such packed lives they easily forget to respond. Most simply forget to reply by the suggested date. If you have not heard from an invited guest by the date stated on the invitation, it is advisable to give a call, a friendly reminder that you are looking forward to seeing him or her. This not only jogs the person's memory, but lets you find out if he or she is planning to attend, and is helpful to both parties.

Create an Entertaining File

Hospitality plus requires that you keep notes on all entertaining that you do. Shown in Appendix A is what I have in mind.[2] You may duplicate this page and keep it in a file. On the second sample are the notes I made after the Christmas party. I recorded who was invited (also list those you asked who did not come), the date, time, type of party, and the menu. Notes about the menu keep you from serving the same food to the same people should you entertain again. Hospitality plus requires that you think up a new menu!

A brief record of what you used for table decorations and centerpieces will help you in two ways: you could reconstruct the same setting again if you could remember what you did previously, or you could change to something else if you have employed that idea before. Notes on games and entertainment as well as what you wore are also helpful. Under personal items record anything you learned about your guests' personal likes and dislikes: Lois doesn't like green peppers; Gene is allergic to wheat, etc.

Keep the Event Moving

It isn't up to the guests to keep a party or gathering moving, but rather you as host. As coordinator of the event, you must see that introductions are made, that people circulate, and that no one gets stuck in a corner with a bore. Your eyes should always be scanning your guests, looking for anyone who needs rescuing from an uncomfortable situation.

Enough preplanning should have taken place that you can be visible at your own event. If you are rushing around setting the table, cooking, mixing, and baking, the more shy and retiring person may not be able to catch up with you. You are the central person all people know, since everyone there may not know everyone else. As host it is up to you to help them meet someone interesting and get a conversation started. Make sure you give people something to talk about as they are introduced!

Once conversations are up and going, please don't interrupt. You may have to when the meal is served, but until then, let people talk without interruption.

Concentrate on Your Guests

If you let food preparation and sensational decorations consume your time and energy, you will likely be an anxious host. And if you are anxious, you will be unable to concentrate on your guests' needs. Make sure that you have done enough preplanning so that when your guests are with you, you can forget yourself and relax—even though you have a meal to serve. Remember, your goal is to extend hospitality and encouragement to your guests—not impress them with your superior entertaining skills.

When you find yourself getting upset or worried over preparations, take time to review your goal: "to offer hospitality and encouragement!" Submit your nervous preparations to the Lord, who says, "Do not be anxious about anything, but in everything, by prayer and petition, with thanksgiving, present your requests to God" (Phil. 4:6, NIV). Ask God to take away your nervousness and thank Him for giving you the guests to whom you wish to minister. It is possible that you could entertain angels unaware.

*When I give,
I give
myself.*

WALT WHITMAN

Give Him your worries about how the house looks, how the food will taste, and all your other concerns about preparation. Set aside your own personal pride in the matter and ask God to make it a comfortable event for you and your guests so that you can offer them the love and encouragement they need. Then let it rest in His hands.

Because they are so important, your guests need more than physical preparation. They need personal attention that you cannot offer if you are rushed and worried over getting everything done.

Keep It Simple

One good thing about entertaining today is that people tend to keep it more relaxed and simple. This makes it easier for both the host and the guests. The simpler you maintain things and the more preplanning you do, the more your guests can relax. And the more guests relax, the more they can enjoy the occasion. There can be true beauty in simplicity, and there is a real art to learning how to serve a simple meal in an elegant style.

Some friends of mine, Dr. and Mrs. Hervey Gimbel, have mastered such artful hospitality. Harry and I have been guests in several of their homes. It doesn't matter whether they live in a 5,000-square-foot mountain chalet, a log cabin, or a condo in southern California, they have the ability to serve simply but elegantly. Both have such a gracious relaxed manner about them that they can serve you bread and tea and you will feel that you have feasted. The bread will likely be homemade and presented on some hand-painted heirloom china. Simple fare always served in a relaxed manner by people who make you feel like a million dollars—what a combination to master!

The Seating of Guests

As host it is up to you to tell guests where to sit when they gather at the table. It is not good enough to say, "Sit wherever you like." In advance you need to think through whom you will position next to and across from each other. Keep in mind that people will talk more with those across from them than those placed next to them.

The importance of seating impressed me the other night when we went out to dinner with friends. Connie was seated to my left and Harry directly across. I enjoy having Harry across from me when we are out to dinner alone, but I spent the entire evening with my neck crooked to the left until it developed a real crick. Harry and Frank talked to each other, and we had two conversational groups going on rather than one. It was an enjoyable evening but could have been even more so had the four of us been able to share the conversation. The incident gave me a valuable lesson that we should not leave seating to chance.

You should not seat husbands and wives next to or across from each other unless it is unavoidable, as in a dinner party for four, where they would naturally be seated next to each other. Even engaged or newly married couples should be seated apart from each other. The reason is that these people supposedly have had time enough to talk to each other. Separating them also gives each a chance to tell shared stories without interruption or contradiction.

Serving the Meal

The host also takes the lead in showing by example how to serve the meal. Plates may be filled in the kitchen if the host is more comfortable with that approach. Using the kitchen will avoid a serving cart, cluttering the table with serving dishes, or having to employ a buffet table. If you prefer, you may place all serving dishes on the table. Or you may keep the serving dishes on a serving cart or sideboard. Unless the host has filled the plates in the kitchen, guests then serve themselves under his or her guidance.

When the candles are out, all women are fair.
PLUTARCH

Having a serving or tea cart leaves you the freedom to stay with your guests throughout the entire meal. All casseroles, platters, and other dishes can be served directly from the tea cart. You can pass serving dishes around the table without cluttering the table. In addition, you can easily observe who might need another serving and pass any dish, since all of them rest beside you on the serving cart.

At the close of the meal, as host you may ask the guests to pass their empty plates to you; then you can place them on the cart's lower shelf. Finally you can wheel the cart to the kitchen area and unload it either immediately or later as desired. This saves endless popping up and down and leaves you free to enjoy your guests and monitor their needs.

I do not have a formal dining room. My home is small and has only a dining-family room combination. But because the space is open, I can extend the table to seat 10 to 12 if necessary. Although there is no room for a serving cart, I do have an antique stand that I transform into a serving area when entertaining. Trivets and serving pads cover the oak wood, and this becomes my serving cart. If you are short of space or money, improvise with a piano bench, card table, or even a TV tray.

Still another way to serve is to place the main course directly in front of your place at the table and serve everyone from there. I use this method on those occasions when the main dish is too large, cumbersome, or hot to pass around the table. Asking my guests to pass each plate to me, I serve and hand the plate back. The other dishes you can pass around the table. This also requires that you as host observe your guests during the meal to know when to offer refills.

Avoid being a guilt-provoking host. When a guest chooses not to eat something or declines seconds, this well-meaning but maddening breed make their guests feel miserable by accusing them of not liking the food or insisting that they gorge themselves beyond capacity.

Entertaining nowadays follows few absolutes. Many people now do not know who Amy Vanderbilt and Emily Post are, or if they did, would not care! To a large extent you can do as you please (within limits). What's important is whether you know what you plan to do and whether it works for you.

The general rules for etiquette and common sense still apply in more uncommon situations. Think through the event and plan in advance, remembering that the comfort of your guests should be paramount. If you make a few mistakes along the way, you will only be like the rest of us.

Conversational Flow

Good conversation is much like a good tennis volley. You toss the ball out and someone else returns it. But a person cannot keep the ball in the air long by himself or herself. Some quieter people are necessary too, as they make good listeners. Good listeners flatter others with thoughtful attention and concentration upon the subject under discussion.

Some people are born good conversationalists, and others have to learn the art. But it is something that can be acquired. For example, good conversation interests most of the people present. At an office party nothing could be more boring to spouses not working at the office than an entire evening devoted to people and events of which they know nothing.

Good conversation is generally of a positive, cheerful, and uplifting nature, as opposed to depressing, sad, and controversial subjects. Nothing is more fun at a gathering of friends than laughter. Everyone enjoys a good laugh. People gravitate to people and places where they can share good clean fun and laughter.

A good conversationalist will learn how to draw people out of their shells with insightful questions. Avoid probing personal questions, but those of a more general nature when asked in a flattering manner will prompt even the shiest and most withdrawn person into a conversation.

As a general rule, if someone asks about your children, it is the time to say they are doing "fine" or "great, thank you." If you do have something of real interest to report, then it is socially acceptable to give such information: "Rodney just graduated from medical school and is taking his residency at Florida Hospital." Or "Susie jumped off the diving board this week and broke her ankle. She's in a cast but is recovering nicely." Such things are newsworthy and might contribute to a new topic of conversation. But to take over the conversation at this point and give all the gruesome details of a recent surgery or brag endlessly about the accomplishments of a child should be reserved for family and closest friends only.

As a guest in someone's home, you can plunge enthusiastically into any conversation. But as host it is essential that you assume a more passive role. After everyone is served, you may want to tell a story to get things rolling. Every host needs to have some stories, jokes, or topics of interest up his or her sleeve in order to perk up a conversation that seems to be going stale. Experience will teach you how to sense when a conversation is about to lag and how to head it off and fill the void. It can be a bit of news obtained from radio or TV, a funny thing that happened at the office, or some inside information about a sporting event.

Anything from politics to controversial topics can be discussed at the table, as long as everyone remembers not to be pompous or overbearing. Operations along with other gore and violence are probably best not discussed at the table. Dinner gatherings are usually designed to be festive occasions, a time to lift people's spirits, to encourage them and make them feel good and happy. Depressing conversation will hardly accomplish such a goal.

It helps to set the scene for good conversation by having low, warm lighting, which usually means turning off glaring overhead lights. The cozy glow of a crackling fire or burning candles also lends a warm coziness to the event. Barely discernible music playing in the background

A word aptly spoken is like apples of gold in settings of silver.
PROVERBS 25:11, NIV

also lends another warm touch. Such music should be instrumental as opposed to singing, which would be distracting.

It is the duty of the host to see that the conversational flow shifts smoothly at the table and that no one gets left out. At a large gathering several conversations might take place around the table. If you feel you are not up to the task of directing conversation, then invite someone who is a gifted conversationalist. Then you won't have to worry about this aspect so much.

Talk About Tables
Something that contributes to good conversation is the shape of the table around which people are eating and visiting. And it's hard to beat a round table. A round table democratically brings everyone together in such a way as to allow each guest to see the others. It

also makes them all equal parts of the group, encouraging general conversation. The traditional rectangular table produces a much more limited equality and vision. Today many homes do not feature a separate formal dining area, but one in which the dining area is part of a family room or larger open area. A round table here lends itself to such surroundings in a more aesthetically pleasing way.

A larger number of people can squeeze around a round table than a rectangular one. It is possible to keep adding guests until no knee room remains. They do not "fall off" the end as with a rectangular table. Crowding around a round table can be a plus, since it promotes closeness and a feeling of camaraderie the minute guests seat themselves.

By recommending a round table I am not implying that it is impossible to get a feeling of camaraderie from another shape of table. However, those who are thinking of investing in a table for the future can keep this point in mind. Many more things go into successful entertaining than the shape of a table, but those whose favorite entertainment is talking around the table should carefully consider this point.

All meals do not have to be eaten in the dining area because the table is there. Most tables can be moved. If your entire backyard is in bloom, creating a spectacular view visible only through the living room windows, why not set up a table there for the meal? And people do not always have to sit evenly around a table. Instead, they could be seated in a crescent to one side. This will encourage them to focus on the view on the opposite side of the table, but at the same time it makes for more difficult conversational flow. If you have a large rectangular table with only a few guests, group them together at one end. This creates a more intimate and congenial atmosphere.

If you cannot seat all your guests at one table, you can obtain more seating by adding another table at one end and extending the length. Or you can set up another table in a nearby area. Card tables come in handy here and usually will seat four more. Or you can improvise tables by purchasing a piece of plywood, cutting it to size, and setting it on sawhorses. You can increase the size of any table by setting a piece of uncut plywood on top of it. Such plywood will allow you to create round, square, and rectangular tables. Doors also make good tables, as do picnic and coffee tables.

On a trip to Russia I visited the home of Leo Tolstoy, the famous Russian novelist. After the tour my new Russian friend, Oleg, invited me to dinner at his home. It was fascinating to see the inside of a Russian home (though it was probably more elite than most). Dinner preparations were in progress, but no one had yet prepared a table. Then my hosts rapidly carried a table—the kitchen table, I presume—to the living room and set it with a cloth and dishes. They collected chairs from around the house, and we shared a meal in an unforgettable and yet charming manner.

You can supplement the seating of large groups with folding chairs stashed in a closet or borrowed from a friend.

Handling Accidents

Even the most careful eater will occasionally have an accident at the table. But both the guest and the host should minimize its significance. Nothing should be said unless it is a major accident that would gain the attention of everyone, such as knocking over a glass of water. Clean up messes as quickly and quietly as possible, thus sparing the feelings of those involved.

An amusing story tells of a young family who invited the new preacher's family for dinner after church. The mother was concerned that all the children be on their best behavior, since she was anxious to make a good impression. The table had her best china, and linen napkins adorned each plate. A lovely centerpiece flanked by lighted candles held everyone's attention.

All bowed their heads as the father asked God's blessing upon the food. When he finished, the 9-year-old girl reached for her glass of iced herbal tea and knocked it over. Little brother jumped to get out of the way of the cascading liquid and knocked his glass over too. An awkward moment of silence reigned as everyone looked at the mother. Disappointment was written all over her face.

Before anyone could say anything, the father flipped over his glass of tea and began to laugh. The preacher caught on and knocked over his glass of tea as he joined in the laughter. The preacher's wife likewise pushed over her glass and giggled. Everyone looked back at the mother, who finally, with an expression of resignation, picked up her glass and dumped the contents on the table.

Everyone roared with laughter. The father gave his daughter a special wink as she laughed in embarrassment. As she winked back, a tear spilled down her face as she looked worshipfully at her father, who had saved her from one of life's most embarrassing moments.[3]

Hospitality plus demands that we be prepared to handle all emergency situations as graciously and with as much tact as did this family.

Should a guest swallow something the wrong way and suffer a choking spell, good manners dictate that others quietly talk among themselves, thereby giving the choking person time to regain composure. Sometimes the choking is serious enough to require a Heimlich maneuver. Food choking is the sixth leading cause of accidental death. It takes only four minutes to die from it unless someone takes immediate action. If someone at your table cannot breathe or becomes pale or cyanotic (blue), the person needs immediate emergency attention.

Handling Potentially Tense Situations

Try as you may to mix people appropriately, what happens when you accidentally put two people together who have opposing views and their conversation goes beyond a "friendly" discussion? As host you can deliberately interrupt and change the subject. You can also break up a discussion heading in that direction by suggesting that everyone move to the living room, patio, poolside, or wherever. Or you might suggest a game.

Also, you may politely say with a smile on your face, "I want everyone to have a good time and enjoy the meal and our time together. I am asking that you continue your conversation at another time and another place."

As host you should see that each guest gets protected from the assaults of another insensitive guest. You did not go to all your effort to have someone else ruin the event. If there develops any chance that someone could destroy the atmosphere of hospitality and encouragement that you are attempting to offer, it is up to you to take control and steer the conversation to a safer subject.

After delivering your little speech, make sure you have a new, safe, and perhaps funny subject to introduce. Humor will break the tension, giving people a chance to laugh and feel good again. Another tactic is to ask one of the guests involved in the potentially controversial discussion to assist you with some task

Blessed are they who can laugh at themselves, for they shall never cease to be amused.

that only he or she could possibly help you with. And make it fast!

I had a close call with such a situation at an election results party that I give every four years during the presidential elections. I had invited a large group of people, all of whom were Republicans except for one couple. A lot of good natured ribbing developed during the meal and during an election game we played following the meal. At first people said everything in good fun, but eventually I overheard some cutting remarks made from time to time. As we continued to watch the election returns roll in, I got slightly worried over a certain tension I was feeling. It was a relief when the one odd couple left early. I sincerely hope they did not depart offended. Next time, before throwing an election party, I will check political persuasions first!

Surviving a Bore

From time to time you'll discover a guest who is a real bore. No need to rend your clothing or take a vow of celibacy over it. One of your goals in extending hospitality is to encourage others. Bores need a lot of encouragement. They would probably prefer not to be bores, but they don't know how to change what they have become.

Many are well-educated persons who simply don't know how to converse or interact with others. So they lecture. A know-it-all attitude and endless details are their stock-in-trade. But by the time they have decided whether it was their third or fourth trip to Hawaii, whether they went to Oahu or Maui first, you (and everyone else present) know what you're in for.

A gracious host survives bores, duds, and many other things. You may feel like uninviting the person, stuffing his or her mouth so full he or she can't talk, or running away. But now is the time for you to put into practice all the attributes of hospitality and graciousness that you've been dying to try. Remember, this is only one event in life. This too shall pass.

---

[1] Suggestions in this chapter are derived from several sources: the author; *The Amy Vanderbilt Complete Book of Etiquette* rev. Letitia Baldridge (Garden City, N.Y.: Doubleday and Co., 1978); *Emily Post's Etiquette,* 14th ed. (New York: Harper and Row, 1984).

[2] Entertainment file idea is adapted from a seminar presented by Emily Barnes.

[3] Len McMillan, *ParentWise* (Hagerstown, Md.: Review and Herald, 1993), p. 134.

Luminaries mark an interesting trail for guests,
or you can surround a picnic site with them, or line a sidewalk.

7

CREATING A SPECIAL ATMOSPHERE

ave you noticed that when you go to someone's home you can almost sense instantly whether it will be a pleasant occasion? What is it about going into a home that gives such a feeling? It is the use of a special touch.*

Special touches make the difference between an ordinary occasion and a memorable one. Often we are unaware of the small things that can make a big difference. But it's small touches that affect our emotions and set a mood—flickering candles and lots of them, a bouquet of fresh flowers, a beautifully set table, soft background music, a crackling fire in the fireplace, the fragrant smell of potpourri, and a relaxed and happy host.

The atmosphere of your home, then, is more important than the food you serve, your table decorations, the centerpiece, or the activities you have planned. The real secret in making the occasion special is to create that special atmosphere that says, "You are welcome here." How is it done?

Lighting

To a large extent the type of lighting that greets guests as they enter a room determines its atmosphere. Lighting requires thoughtful and creative use in order to obtain the best effect.

The intensity of light in any area determines how people relate to each other. If you are having a group over who do not know one another and you want them to mingle, mix, and get acquainted, turn up all the lights. Bright lights make people more talkative. After the evening gets under way and you want people to quiet down a bit, however, lower the lights.

Radio City Music Hall learned this the hard way when they opened in New York City. The loud, animated conversation in the foyer disturbed the patrons in the auditorium. The management called in a lighting consultant. His solution? Dim all lights in the large public areas that had been brightly lit to show off the new modern design and murals. To this day the wattage in public areas is so meager you practically trip over the furniture, but rarely do you hear a sound above a whisper!

At a children's or fifties' party the lighting should be bright to set a lively mood. Subdued lighting is more appropriate at other gatherings. If you experiment with lighting, you'll find the principle works.

The best light to have in the dining area is a general source that you can regulate. You can add a dimmer switch to any light. The overall light needs to be balanced, and then you can accent with pools of brighter but softer light. Candles make a great choice here.

If you would have your home sweet and inviting, make it bright with air and sunshine.

ELLEN WHITE

Lighting throughout the guest area should match, at least to a degree, the mood you are attempting to create. I tend to favor Touch lamps because with a flick of the finger you can adjust the level of light. Lighted candles throughout the house also create a special atmosphere that says "You are welcome here." Scented votive candles placed around a room mask unpleasant cooking odors and give a pleasing aroma. When serving a Chinese meal, I always burn incense. A roaring fire in the fireplace not only gives off warmth, but sends a friendly message that sets a tone for the occasion. Whatever lighting you use indoors should always be bright enough so guests can see rugs, stairs, and steps up and down.

Candle Magic

Flickering candles with shifting shadows create a festive mood for special occasions and holidays. Candlelight gives a uniqueness to the occasion, providing a warm and welcome glow. People look younger and more romantic and alluring in the glow of a candle. You can capture and expand the magic of candlelight through creative use of candles and candleholders in assorted shapes, sizes, and color.

Here are some ideas on how to employ candles creatively. Use them to spark your own creativity.

- A candelabra or a cluster of candles gives an intimate, almost glamorous feel to a dinner table.
- Set a bushy ivy plant in a basket and insert six to eight tall taper candles into the soil. Use as a centerpiece.
- Place three glass hurricane shades down the center of your table. Fill the bottom of the shades with a three- to four-inch mixture of fresh cranberries and unshelled almonds. In the center of each shade insert a three-inch-column candle of a color that enhances your color scheme.
- With a vegetable centerpiece of zucchini, yellow squash, cauliflower, carrots, beets, etc., use bell peppers as candleholders. Hollow out the center of each pepper just enough so that it will hold a votive candle. Spot several of them around your edible centerpiece.
- Arrange red or green apples in a wicker basket. Tuck in sprigs of ivy or green leaves to cover "empty spots." Select two or more apples as candleholders. Hollow out the ends and insert votive or taper candles. It is perfect for a country-look centerpiece.

- Accent a veggie theme with the stalks of a celery heart. Using any empty eight-ounce can, line celery stalks up side by side around the outside of the can with edges touching the bottom of the can. Secure them in place with wire and a ribbon to accent your color scheme. Place a column candle inside the can and light. Your guests will love it.

- Votive candles in small clear glass containers scattered around a centerpiece have real eye appeal. Or if you have enough votive candles and containers, one placed in front of each place setting is stunning.

- Candles floating in a low, clear glass container can be striking. Float a flower in the midst of the candles—camellias, magnolia blossoms, or a large rose would be perfect.

- Place a grouping of three-inch candles inside a fireplace that is not in use. You can cluster 6, 12, 18, or more column candles together to produce a striking effect. Fresh greenery or boughs placed around the candles add a finishing touch.

- If you live near a Cost Plus chain store, look for a column candle made by General Wax Company. It has "wells" around the outside for liquid wax to drain into, allowing the candle to burn more evenly. These candles are available in many colors and heights and are my personal favorite.

- Freeze your tapers before burning them, and they will not drip wax onto your table. Don't ask me why—I can't explain it. I only know it works.

Note: Whereas candlelight lends a romantic glow and a festive appearance to the table, it alone may not be enough light to eat by comfortably. Combining it with low lighting may prove more comfortable. You don't want your guests groping blindly for their silver, or spilling, dropping, and knocking things over because they can't see. A dimmer switch or rheostat installed on the light switch will allow you to lower and adjust the light to capture the perfect glow. Hint: Pink light bulbs also produce a warm rosy feeling.

Outdoor Lighting

Some creative lighting touches can be added outside your home to set a mood, enhance decor, or carry out a theme.

- A string or two of clear twinkling Christmas lights in a tree gives a special effect.
- A string or two of brightly colored patio lights hung around a patio or eating area creates a colorful and festive atmosphere.
- Tiki torches can also be used for a special effect, especially if you are having a Hawaiian luau.
- Hurricane shades over candles will protect candles from being blown out by the wind when dining outdoors.
- Citronella candles will repel insects, but they give off a slightly unpleasant odor that forces a choice between insects or the odor.

'was her thinking
of others
that made you
think of her.
ELIZABETH BROWNING

- Night lighting is easy with paper bags. Take a lunch-sized bag and turn down the top two to three times to form a collar. Then fill the bag one third full of sand to support a candle. These luminaries mark an interesting trail for guests, or you can surround a picnic site with them or line a driveway.

With all the special effects you are trying to capture and use creatively, don't forget commonsense lighting. Check to make sure that you have a well-lit path between your home and your guests' cars.

Music! Music! Music!

Just as lighting sets one portion of the mood, so also does music. Not only does it help to create a special atmosphere but it also helps to eliminate awkward silences during introductions while you are trying to get conversations up and running. The volume should be up a little when guests first arrive and lowered as the noise level rises.

The type of music played will also depend on the occasion.

Instrumental music is preferable. Since you probably won't have time to be changing compact discs or cassettes and deciding what you would like to play next, you should take time beforehand to think through the mood you want to create.

Theme entertaining provides even more opportunities for the creative home disk jockey. For a Mexican patio party you can accent a more festive mood with Latin music. A spaghetti supper calls for the strains of guitar music. An evening with a Russian flavor calls for haunting melodies in a minor key. When serving a Chinese meal, I play Oriental music.

As women arrive at my home for a Ladies Night Out meeting, I have sacred instrumentals in the background. Music always plays softly in the background in my home. I use it to set a mood for me. I have lively secular music while I am vacuuming, and sacred background instrumentals during personal devotions.

Use your judgment about the desirability of music. But if you use it, make sure it is suited to the occasion and adjusted to a desirable volume. If you don't have time to watch the volume, assign this task to a youngster. And the auto reverse button now available on some stereo equipment is worth the price in my estimation.

Music can add a lot to an evening's entertainment, but it can also conflict with what you are attempting to create. When played loud enough to be listened to and appreciated, it can make conversation difficult. Loud music is always distracting and never advisable. The volume should never be so loud that guests have to shout at each other or otherwise find it difficult to hear.

Greet Guests Warmly

After adjusting the music and lighting to the mood you wish to create, the next step is a warm welcome at the door from both hosts. This means that you must have all preparations so well under control that you can personally greet each guest. A warm personal greeting shows how delighted you are to have them in your home.

Not only should you greet each guest personally as he or she enters your home, but hospitality plus suggests that you speak to them by name. In addition, if it suits your personality, you can give them an affectionate touch—a handshake, a touch on the shoulder or arm, or a hug—all appropriate to your relationship to the guest. Your greeting should communicate, "You are a very special person, and I am delighted to have you here."

Recently a couple who were seminar coordinators welcomed me into their home. After the husband picked me up at the airport, his wife greeted me at the door. "Nancy, we have waited so long for you to be with us. Welcome to our home." She gave me a warm embrace, and I instantly sensed it was going to be a special occasion. And it was unforgettable. The initial welcome at the door set the tone for what followed.

Introduce Guests Creatively

Once you have welcomed your guests and taken their wraps, introductions come next. I have little interest in what Emily Post says about whether the older person should be presented to the younger or vice versa. Protocol is of lesser importance than mixing people who may not know each other. An introduction could be perfectly correct, but unless two persons who do not know each other are given some common ground about which they can communicate, the introduction is a failure.

The secret to a good introduction, then, is to include a short remark about the person. "Joan, I want you to meet Claudia, a very talented pianist. Claudia, Joan is the first-grade teacher at the school." Or "John, this is Peter Jacobson, a building contractor. Peter, John is an avid basketball fan." In both cases, I have introduced two topics for conversation. Each has something to build on.

Introductions are simple when you throw away protocol and include something of interest about the person for the sake of helping others make conversation. The minute a conversation begins to move, everyone can relax.

Provide Comfortable Seating

You can get conversations started, but keeping them going has a lot to do with comfortable seating. From here on out, the key to a warm and friendly environment is the arrangement of furniture. Informal groupings of chairs and sofas that face each other are excellent.

In my home I have two matching sofas facing each other. Buying two sofas rather than one is double the money but worth the investment. At one end of both sofas I have a love seat. So the grouping of three forms a U shape. People can see and talk with those directly across from them or next to them on the love seat. Such a grouping has also proved to be excellent for the monthly Lady's Night Out women's ministry group that meets in my home.

Never set a chair off in a corner by itself or someone is sure to face the event alone. Worse yet, someone could stand over them talking down to them. Another thing to avoid is a long sofa with a long coffee table in front of it. It is difficult for those seated in a long row to converse with each other and even more difficult for others to get to them around the long coffee table. Furthermore, it is next to impossible for anyone caught in the middle of the row to make an easy exit. The individual may find himself or herself trapped there for a long time. We don't want to give guests the impression that they are in jail. They must have the freedom to move about when necessary.

You can move your furniture to provide groupings of chairs that will promote conversation. Chairs should be close enough so that two or more people can visit without raising their voices or shouting across a room to be heard.

Plan Entertainment for Children

If you have children in the home, it is probably easier for you to entertain families with children. Your children will likely be delighted with someone else to play with. Entertainment of children in this case will most likely take care of itself as your children escort guest children to their room to play.

Some of the rest of you may have a mental block about entertaining children, along with many excuses. "My house isn't child-proof. . . . Kids make me nervous. . . . Let families with kids entertain their own friends," etc. The truth of the matter is that guests will not feel welcome if you are nervously jumping around snatching items out of a child's hands while cautioning, "Please don't touch that. It could get broken." No one can relax when you can't relax.

If you entertain a family with children, and I surely hope you do, the answer to what to do with children when you don't have any of your own is to keep a basket or box of toys on hand—just for the kids' sake. A game, coloring book and crayons, a doll, a couple of neat cars, and a book or two generally solves the problem. They may not be new toys, but they are new to the visiting children and can easily hold their attention until the meal is ready.

Several ideas may be helpful when serving children. A high chair or a booster chair is a great aid for small children. Sometimes I serve children at a separate table from the adults, depending on the occasion, how many children there are, and who the children are. I take every effort, even though the children are at a separate table, to make their table look special and treat them as guests, not as second-class citizens who are really a bother. If the children are eating over carpet where food spills might be a catastrophe, I may put a sheet or plastic tablecloth on the floor under the table so the parents, children, and I can relax and enjoy the meal. I would not bother with this when children are eating over a floor that you can easily mop up.

When you seat children at the main table with adults, use the clear plastic tablecloth trick. This way you can set your table in any elegant manner you desire, and it remains indestructible. Ordinarily, Battenberg lace and children would be incompatible. But all you would have to do to childproof expensive and difficult-to-care-for Battenberg lace is to cover it with lightweight clear plastic available at most fabric and hardware stores. But I don't employ the clear plastic only when entertaining children—I employ it every time I use Battenberg lace (and other times, too). It makes less work for me, others relax more, and I entertain more frequently because it is less work.

My daughter Carlene and her husband moved to a new area and visited a new church. Afterward she told me she had prepared dinner for company but couldn't find anyone to invite home. "Why should you invite company for dinner?" I chided. It was her first visit to this church, and the church should have been extending invitations to her family. "Mom," she explained patiently, "when you have four children, no one ever invites you home for dinner."

Her words struck me with force. Carlene and Brian get invited out to dinner with friends and professional colleagues. But never as a family. My daughter has worked hard to train her sons in appropriate behavior. The boys have used goblets since they were 2 or 3 so as to learn how to handle them and not take a bite from one like a friend's child did! Carlene buys cheap goblets at Wal-Mart and has replaced them many times, but they know how to use them. Yet they rarely get to use their manners at the homes of others because no one wants to invite a family with four boys over.

It is a tragedy that families with children automatically get crossed off a prospective guest list with no further consideration. Could this be one of the reasons that more of these families are not staying with the church? "Inasmuch as you have done it unto one of the least of these, you have done it unto me," Christ said. Let us rethink our priorities and open our homes to families with children. A little advance planning will solve most problems, and the parents will greatly appreciate your efforts.

Dress Appropriately for the Occasion

Today's relaxed lifestyle reflects itself in more relaxed clothing. Some can only on rare occasions be motivated beyond jeans and a sweatshirt. If you intend to have a fancy dinner party and expect people to be formally dressed, you are going to have to let them know. It is up to you as host to inform guests what the occasion is and what type of dress it calls for.

More casual dress is expected at a patio or poolside party, a picnic, or an outdoor barbecue. But dress-up occasions are few and far between for most of middle-class America. You must let guests know what you expect of their dress.

You, as host, must also dress appropriately for the occasion. If you are either overdressed or underdressed, it could provide some uncomfortable moments for the guest as he or she realizes that the expectation was for the opposite attire. I would also suggest that you choose clothing that is comfortable with sleeves short enough so that cuffs do not dip into food, as well as clothing easy to clean should you splatter or spill while preparing food. You also need to think through color and overall theme when selecting what you wear. A red hostess gown may look striking, but would overpower a table adorned in pink rosebuds.

Keep the Conversation Flowing

An accomplished host knows how to tuck tidbits of information away for recall at just the time needed. As you hear something on radio or TV that would be of general interest to others, jot it down. When reading about medicine, gardening, travel, or something interesting in the Dear Abby column, cut it out and save it for a future get-together. Cute jokes can be invaluable. For example, have you heard the one about the little girl who asked her grandmother how old she was?

"Honey," Grandma responded, "you shouldn't ask people that question."

"Well," the girl replied, "how much do you weigh?"

"Honey, that's another question you shouldn't ask grown-ups. It isn't polite," her grandmother chided.

The next day the little girl was back with a big smile on her face. "Grandma, I know how old you are. You're 62, and you weigh 140 pounds."

Astonished, Grandma asked how she knew that.

"I found your driver's license and read it," the girl replied. "But Grandma, I found out something else about you. On your driver's license it said you got an F in sex."

A joke like this or some other tidbit about a current event can trigger good conversation. Such topics are of general interest to most people. Again, it is up to you to keep the conversation flowing without dominating it. Because you are not the star of the event, you should not do all the talking, but instead learn to draw your guests out. Work on your listening skills.

> *A good laugh is sunshine in a house.*
> THACKERAY

When mixing Christians with non-Christians, remember that non-Christians generally start and carry conversations easier than Christians do. Generally speaking, they have had more practice in social situations and are more accepting of others than Christians who tend to judge more critically by certain standards. Non-Christians more easily include newcomers into their groups and appear more skilled at "small talk."

Christians stick closer to their cliques and have more difficulty reaching out to newcomers. Since they do not do as much mixing in social circles, they feel more uncomfortable with it.

Our goal is to get the two groups moving toward each other rather than avoiding each other. The objective is to get good conversations started so friendship can be built on it. An accomplished host knows how to stimulate and direct conversation.

Creating a Special Atmosphere for Overnight Guests

Occasionally our homes must accommodate overnight guests. How can we best extend hospitality to make someone comfortable and welcome when away from home? According to bed-and-breakfast innkeepers, having a large and lavishly furnished guest room isn't always the ticket to making guests feel welcome. It's the special touches. Some essentials that make the stay pleasant:

- Proper sheets and bedding. All hosts should sleep in their own guest rooms or beds once before they ask someone else to. See if the mattress is lumpy and what blankets the visitor will need. New decorator sheets that reflect the decor of the room are a nicety but not a necessity.
- Adequate heat and/or ventilation. Do windows open with ease? Is a fan or air-conditioning needed?
- A clean wastebasket in both the guest room and bathroom.
- A good reading light by the bed.
- Closet space with a few empty hangers.
- A notepad and pen on the bedside table.
- A clock radio so guests can set an alarm and know what is going on in the world.
- A water glass.

Extra touches:

- A bouquet of fresh flowers or a pretty plant.
- A small TV set.
- A good book or magazine.
- A container of goodies, such as special candies, mints, or other treats.
- An extra pillow for sitting up in bed to read.

The guest bathroom should include such necessities as:

- A fresh bar of soap in the sink, tub, or shower area.
- A shower cap.
- A fresh bath towel, face towel, and two washclothes for each guest, along with a towel rack on which to hang towels.

- A bath mat for the floor after bathing.
- A hook on the back of the bathroom door to hang bathrobes, etc.
- Sufficient facial and toilet tissue.

Bed-and-breakfast innkeepers suggest the following extra touches:

- The scent of potpourri in a pretty container.
- An afghan or quilt tossed over a chair.
- A stack of current magazines.
- Shiny, reflective things of silver, brass, colored glass, and crystal to literally make rooms sparkle.
- A game or puzzle laid out on a table.

The manner of giving shows the character of the giver more than the gift itself.
LAVATER

- Sheet music on the piano (it looks "homey" and invites a musician to play, and encourages sing-alongs).
- A guest book for people to "sign in." Take a Polaroid picture of each guest and affix it to their page. Some guest books have Bible verses on the page that would act as a silent witness.

Many groups have welcomed me warmly and gone the extra mile in making me feel comfortable even in a motel—my home away from home. But no one has excelled in the spirit of hospitality so freely offered as a group of women in Pendleton, Oregon.

Prior to my arrival they placed a bouquet of fresh irises in the room. In addition, they had left a white basket of unbelievable goodies—red and green apples, nectarines, grapes, cookies, chocolate kisses, muffins, and a packet of orange spice tea. All of this they had tucked prettily in lavender tissue paper with some hard candies scattered here and there. To top it off, they had included a bottle of Wild Cherry Clearly Canadian. And get this—a votive candle and holder for atmosphere! With this type of welcome I knew it was going to be an unforgettable weekend, and it was.

*The ideas in this chapter are from several sources, including the author and the Hospitality Seminars offered. Other ideas are adapted from Carole Collier, *Serving Food With Style* (Garden City, N.Y.: Doubleday and Co., 1981).

The more unique and attractive the thank-you note you write, the more memorable you become in the minds of your hosts.

ON BEING A GOOD GUEST

eing invited to someone's home is always an honor and a privilege. The more effort, time, and preparation that has gone into preparing to receive you as a guest, the more of an honor it is. But regardless of whether it is a long-planned-for or an impromptu event, when someone opens their home and invites you to partake of their hospitality, it requires something from you as a guest.*

RSVPs
If you have received a written invitation with an RSVP (French for "Please reply"), good manners dictate that you respond by the specified date, if not before. When someone extends a verbal invitation, respond enthusiastically. "Thank you so much for thinking of me/us. I/We would be happy to join you." If you must check with a spouse's schedule, say so and then call back with a definite answer so your potential host can make definite plans. An "iffy" response is rude and unfair.

When the event occurs, make every effort to arrive on time—not early or late, but on time. If you come early, your host may not yet be dressed or quite ready. It may be socially acceptable in some circles to arrive a few minutes late—no one seems to want to be the first one there trying to get the party up and functioning. But that isn't your responsibility anyway. That's the host's problem. Your responsibility is to be there within 15 to 20 minutes of the stated time so as not to cause stress for your host.

Host Gifts

Depending on the occasion, you might wish to plan a gift for your host. It can be anything from nuts to a tin of cookies or a jar of homemade jam. For some people, bringing a gift is as natural as breathing. A friend of mine rarely meets me for lunch or any visit without some small surprise—two cookies, a muffin, some herbs from her garden, a miniature vase of violets. This isn't a necessity, but a nicety. If the family has children, and especially if you are staying overnight, plan a surprise for them. Note: a gift does not replace a thank-you note.

Talk About Talking

While it is the duty of the host to see that the conversational flow shifts smoothly at the table and that no one gets left out, it is out of place and rude for a guest to dominate. It is equally rude to spend the entire evening chatting with the one on the right while ignoring the person on the left. Being a good conversationalist demands that sometime during the meal you speak to the persons on both sides of you. This is true even if you are having a fascinating conversation with a particular person and especially if the other individual has been left out and has no one to talk with.

Tact is the ability to close your mouth before somebody else wants to.

A guest of honor, or even the most popular guest, should not talk at length about himself or herself all the while hogging or dominating the spotlight. A good conversationalist will listen as well as talk.

Shoptalk can ruin any gathering unless everyone present participates in the same business or activity. A doctor's wife recently entertained her husband's entire office staff and their spouses. All the staff had worked together for years and had much to talk about. They spent the entire evening telling office stories of which four others had no part. Repeatedly the wife attempted to change or divert the topic, to no avail. She felt the evening was a total failure because of the topic of conversation—shoptalk. Refrain from making this mistake yourself at any gathering.

Table Manners

Should you feel a sneeze coming on at the table, stifle it as best you can by covering your nose and mouth with your napkin. Never blow your nose on the napkin! Should you need to leave the table for a moment, say "Excuse me, please" to your host, take care of your errand, and return to your place, murmuring a quiet apology. Then forget it. The incident does not have to be a big deal unless you make it so.

If someone asks a question when your mouth is full, naturally you must wait until you have chewed much of the food before replying. It is possible, however, to speak with some food in your mouth without being offensive. Hopefully the person asking the question will recognize the dilemma he or she has put you in and give you time to answer or cover until you can speak.

Should food wedge in your teeth and you cannot dislodge it with your tongue, please do not attempt to loosen it with your finger or a toothpick in front of others. If it becomes unbearable, excuse yourself from the table briefly, take care of it out of public view, and then return. People with chronic problems should carry toothpicks with them and use them discreetly.

When a burp threatens to erupt, cover your nose and mouth with your napkin and attempt to muffle the sound as best you can. Then quietly say to no one in particular, "Excuse me!" Should you continue to burp, excuse yourself from the table until the attack subsides.

If a guest near you inadvertently burps in your presence, the polite thing to do is to pretend you did not hear it unless you are in a group of old friends where a good amount of teasing may take place. A thoughtful host or friend will immediately introduce an interesting topic to get everyone talking again and attention diverted from the suffering guest. The silences that follow someone's embarrassment are miserable moments for everyone. Try to minimize them.

You should always treat a host's property with respect. Keep from getting so relaxed in someone else's house that you put your feet on their furniture. And don't tip chairs back on their rear legs if you want to be asked back again.

While you may want to help the host or keep her company, don't follow her to the kitchen unless asked. At a casual dinner with friends you may ask if you can assist, but don't make a nuisance of yourself. If she says yes and has a specific job for you, go ahead. At a more formal dinner you shouldn't even ask.

The same rules apply when cleaning up after a meal. Only with close friends or family should you ever just pop up to help. It may make her nervous to have you in the kitchen. Let her do things her way. You can let people help you in your kitchen if you wish, but you are a guest in her home now.

Following dinner, if the host suggests a planned activity, accept these plans with enthusiasm even if it is not something high on your priority list. You are a guest and must act like one, fitting into the host's plans even if you don't feel like it. Whatever you are asked to do at this point, as graciously as possible attempt to fit in and have a good time. Do your utmost to be accommodating to anything suggested.

Don't stay too late. Even if your host asks you to remain a little longer, you must weigh the advantages and disadvantages. If the party or event is in full swing and no one else has left, feel free to stay. Likewise, leaving early can disturb the mix of people. When one group departs, it seems to signal that everyone should go. It is hard to get the right mix or activity going again when someone has left.

Thank-yous

Anytime someone entertains you in their home for a meal or overnight, it deserves a written note of thanks. The best time to write that thank-you is immediately following the event, but never later than five or six days unless you are on a trip and have not yet returned home. Even then, I recommend taking thank-you notes as you travel. When I am traveling internationally and know it might be as long as two to three weeks before I return home, I carry thank-you notes with me. Sometimes I leave the completed notes on a pillow. Other times I give one of my books as a thank-you with a few warm words of appreciation written inside.

This communicating of one's self to one's friend works two contrary effects; for it redoubleth joys, and cutteth griefs in half.
FRANCIS BACON

Calling afterward and delivering a verbal thank-you is only second best and the easy way out. The best thing to do is to purchase some attractive note paper and handwrite a few words of appreciation. Store-bought cards with a printed message are for the illiterate unless you add your own message to the existing one.

Your thank-you should not be trite: "Thanks for having me over. I really enjoyed myself." First, I hope you enjoyed more than "myself." Your hosts had you over to enjoy them, a meal, and a good time. Compliment her on her cooking and him on a funny story he told. Refer to a guest who fascinated you and the beautiful table decor. Be specific with whatever you mention. When thanking someone for a weekend, a note isn't enough. You should fill a page or two of stationery with pleasant reminiscences and observations about the meals, activities, thoughtful gestures, and hospitality.

Each thank-you note should include several ingredients. Once you have learned them, you can check them off when writing a note to make sure you have included each one. A well-written thank-you note should include:

- Everyone who had a part in entertaining you, not only the host.
- Thanks from all in the family who were recipients of the hospitality.
- Something noteworthy about the event—food particularly enjoyed, a centerpiece, a funny story.
- A remark about the warm hospitality received.

The following note serves as an example of what you might say:

"Dear Don and Lois:

"Thank you so much for including us in your holiday gathering. The invitation to enjoy your hospitality when none of our family could be present was deeply appreciated.

"I particularly enjoyed the privilege of using your new and elegant Thanksgiving dishes. It was a delight to be seated at such a lovely table with your family and warm congenial friends. We enjoyed Dave's company and the report about his recent trip to Johannesburg. Sonny was charming and Amanda an excellent server.

"There's no doubt about the fact that the two of you are experts at the art of making guests feel welcome. We were delightfully spoiled. Many thanks to both of you from both of us.

"Affectionately,

"Harry and Nancy"

The more unique and attractive the note you write, the more memorable you become in the minds of your hosts.

If you are the guest of honor at such an occasion and know how much work your hosts have gone to, it would be a nice gesture to offer a toast with whatever is before you—water, punch, or even milk. In your toast enumerate all the delightful elements you are enjoying. Entertaining is a lot of work, and the least you can do is let people know you appreciate it.

It is not out of place to give a host who has done an outstanding job of making her table look beautiful and serving outstanding food, outstanding accolades. She worked for it, and she deserves it! Please exclaim over it, compliment her, enjoy it, and let her know you do. If her china is particularly beautiful, it is perfectly acceptable to pick it up and turn it over to see the markings. Hopefully she didn't purchase it at K Mart and won't feel obligated to tell you so.

A Word to Overnight Guests

Being a guest in someone's home overnight requires all the previous suggestions for excellent guest relations in addition to a few more:

- Spend time in advance packing everything needed so you don't arrive having to borrow everything from swimsuits to tennis rackets.

- Arrive on time with decent-looking luggage rather than looking like a pack of gypsies with shopping bags and cardboard boxes. If you don't have proper luggage, either purchase or borrow it.

*Do not save
your loving speeches
For your friends
'til they are dead.
Do not write them on
their tombstones
Speak them rather
now instead.*

- If you or someone in your family is not feeling well, cancel your visit.

- Under no circumstances should you ever bring a pet with you. A friend told me recently that when relatives came to visit her for five days they brought a monkey even when asked not to. Monkeys take more care than an infant and smell worse, too! Bringing a pet is sure to cause problems even if your host has enthusiastically told you it is OK.

- If your children accompany you, discipline them carefully, keeping them under control at all times. Under no circumstances should you attempt to discipline your host's children.

- Make your own breakfast and clean up afterward.
- If your host has planned an activity for you to enjoy, accept the plans graciously even if it doesn't sound interesting to you.
- Don't be late for anything, much less everything. Getting meals and organizing sightseeing trips is difficult enough. Do your part by being ready on time.
- If something gets broken during your visit, don't try to hide or ignore it. Tell your host and attempt to replace it or make amends.
- Don't overuse the telephone or, worse yet, make long-distance calls without reimbursing the host for them.
- Relieve your host from preparing a meal by taking him or her out to eat.
- Never stay beyond your projected visit even if invited to do so. An old saying declares that fish and relatives smell after three days. Take this to heart if you want to get invited back again.
- Send a warm note of thanks and a thank-you gift after you leave.

When There Is No Separate Guest Room

If you are a guest in a home without a guest room and will be sleeping on a couch or sleeper sofa, you must make extra effort to be thoughtful. It is difficult for both hosts and guests to live through such stays. Here are a few suggestions to make it more comfortable for both of you:

- Go to bed when the rest of the family retires.
- Fit into breakfast and bathroom schedules cooperatively.
- Fold sheets and blankets and convert the sofa back to being a sofa in the morning.
- Use your suitcase as a bureau and do not unpack what you do not immediately need.
- Leave the area you are using neat and orderly every morning.

- Leave the bathroom neat—fold or hang towels; clean ring off the bathtub; put cosmetics and shaving utensils away. And don't leave the toilet seat up!

---

*Source material on good manners and etiquette is adapted from *The Amy Vanderbilt Complete Book of Etiquette* and *Emily Post's Etiquette.*

*Every homemaker needs to have supplies on hand
for at least one impromptu menu should unexpected guests arrive.*

9

SHORTCUTS, QUICK FIXES

ost of us don't entertain more often simply because we don't have more time. But if we could learn shortcuts that would save us time, we might be able to entertain more frequently. One of my most popular seminars is "Personalized Home Organization Through Order, Joy, and Elegance," in which I teach seven secrets to sanity for stressed women. Through this seminar many people have learned how to get their acts together at home as they organize all the complicated demands on their time. Let me share some shortcuts that will save your sanity for getting ready for company.*

Shortcut 1

Clean after company leaves rather than before they come.

This is possible, of course, only if you have a system of keeping your house orderly week by week. It is a waste of time to vacuum before company comes. The minute your guests walk on your carpet they will leave it covered with shadows. Few guests check out the carpets anyway.

What people notice when they enter the home (after the greeting) is orderliness. Your home can welcome people if it has order instead of clutter. Whether the windows are spotless, the furniture polished or dusted, carpet vacuumed, draperies just back from the cleaners, floors stripped and polished—no. What they will notice is the general appearance—does this home welcome them? If it is clutter-free, it appears to be a clean home.

Rooms should look effortless and have an ease about them that soothes.

It took me years to learn this secret, and I could have saved myself much grief if someone had taught me it long ago. I have a personal daily plan that I follow: Mondays I clean the kitchen; Tuesdays I wash; Wednesdays I do bathrooms, plan menus, and grocery-shop; Thursdays I vacuum; and Fridays I dust. Presto. I can be ready for company almost any day of the week as long as I follow my personal daily plan and don't allow other things to control me. Rather than devoting one day a week to cleaning, I have portioned it out over a week's time. This calls for a different standard of cleanliness. It is never "clean" all in one day, but I maintain a level of cleanliness I can live with all week. And it saves my sanity and allows me to be ready to entertain more frequently.

Shortcut 2
Do as much ahead of time as possible.

Once you get a personal daily plan in effect and your total life becomes more orderly, you can then plan for one or two weeks in advance rather than just allowing the events of each day to control you. When menu planning, you can purchase and prepare foods for future meals and then freeze them. If you know in advance that you will have company after church, you can do a few things ahead of time so that you will have little else to do except set the table. I even do that beforehand, since I want to be able to enjoy my guests once they get to my home.

Getting things done in advance makes the day of entertaining a breeze. Nothing can be more satisfying than being able to take a nap before your guests arrive!

Shortcut 3
Collect recipes that you can prepare in advance.

Forget foods like soufflés that require last-minute preparation; instead, go for the easy stuff. I have a collection of trustworthy standby menus that look great and taste terrific but require a minimum of last-minute preparation. Using the recipes frequently, I make the main dish a week or more ahead of time and freeze it. The dinner rolls and dessert are also frozen. The vegetable, which I purchase fresh, I will prepare in advance and toss into a plastic bag ready for the steamer. I prefer molded salads to tossed salads for company meals, since they too can be made beforehand. Even the veggies for a relish dish you can do ahead of time, arrange on a beautiful platter, and cover with plastic wrap to await their last-minute entry.

I am not a gourmet cook, but I can serve meals that people truly enjoy eating and rave about because I stay with what I know I can handle. If I find myself standing over the sink with aching feet and sore shoulders, I know that somewhere I have lost control of my time and have not done enough prior to the event.

Shortcut 4
Use all the offers for help that come your way.

I save certain tasks for guests to do in case they offer to help. Pleasant tasks like pouring water in glasses, tossing a salad, cutting a pie, decorating the top of a molded salad, and lighting candles give guests something to do and make them feel at home.

You might be able to do it all alone without help from others, but think through the consequences of what you are saying to your children when you refuse help. Children watching you entertain learn that you do not need nor expect their help. They also fail to acquire valuable lessons in food presentation as well as pick up the concept that they are to be served but are not to serve others. Thus they lose valuable experience in cooperative living.

Shortcut 5
Serve more potluck menus.

When serving a full meal, don't be above allowing people who offer to bring part of it to help. I generally prefer to do it alone the first time I entertain guests. After that, they become "part of the family," and if they offer, I accept. Usually I fix the main dish, as they are my specialty. If only one other couple is coming, they might bring dessert and dinner rolls, while I'll prepare the main dish, vegetable, and salad. Having someone take care of the dessert removes a tremendous load off my shoulders. If three families are coming, each can still contribute something.

The real test of your religion is your treatment of those who can be of no possible service to you.

Shortcut 6
Use clear plastic over tablecloths when necessary.

Plastic isn't needed every time you entertain, but it can save a lot of work when using a cloth or mats that require special care. However, I do use it over Battenberg lace every time, and I would always use plastic when children are eating at the table. This means less worry and less cleanup afterward.

Surprise Entertaining

One day after church Harry and I had just gotten home and I was preparing a simple and scanty meal for the two of us. Just then I noticed two cars drive up to our house. A group of people, including a close friend and her new husband, proceeded to our front door. I had invited them to dinner—but for the following week! Obviously we had gotten our wires crossed. Harry and I welcomed them with dazed smiles. We made a split-second decision not to reveal the mistake, as we did not want the new husband to feel that his first venture into our social circle was a disaster.

After a warm welcome, introductions, and a little chitchat with half of me in agonized terror and the other half of me suppressing a hysterical giggle fit, I excused myself to prepare a meal for six rather than two. Fortunately I had an emergency meal on hand. I headed for the freezer, where I had frozen stuffed pasta shells, green peas, and seasoned French bread. With the help of a microwave I got the rock-hard shells thawed some, poured some Ragu spaghetti sauce over them, and sprinkled it with cheese. In 15 minutes the aroma of baking pasta wafted through the air.

Then I set about preparing the table that I ordinarily would have had set in advance, and brought out the emergency centerpiece. (In this case it was an arrangement of dried roses, hydrangea, and yarrow.) With the table set, the main dish in the oven, bread thawing, and peas in the steamer, all I needed to worry about was the salad, which fortunately I had on hand.

At this point I took a breather and showed the guests through my home. While they enjoyed looking over my quilts and Russian mementoes, the aroma of baking pasta permeated the air. The longer it cooked, the more tempting it became. After the tour I prepared the tossed salad, and by the time my surprise guests sat down their appetite had peaked. To this day I don't think they know how surprised I was to see them.

Impromptu Menus

Every homemaker needs to have supplies on hand for at least one impromptu menu should unexpected guests arrive. I'm still licking wounds from a hard-learned lesson I had when I wasn't prepared. Harry was finishing his last year of seminary training. We were dirt-poor—so poor the local church brought us a food basket at Thanksgiving, and we were too grateful to protest.

After church one day I was preparing a meager meal for Harry and two babies when I heard a knock at the door. There stood wealthy friends of my parents, visiting from the West Coast. While I insisted they stay for dinner, my mind frantically searched for an answer to the dilemma I faced. My cupboards did not have enough food to put together a company meal of any description. Without our guests' knowledge I ran from door to door in the large apartment house where we lived, borrowing a little here and a little there until I had a meal. I hid everything in my apron and had to make a couple of trips. Although my guests said nothing to indicate they caught on to my plight, they did take us out for supper! It was a difficult experience.

Should guests pop in on you unexpectedly, you should always have on hand one emergency meal that you can throw together rapidly. Decide on a sample menu that will work for you and tuck all ingredients on a high shelf or in the freezer away from the easy reach of family members. Should any ingredients get borrowed, replace them immediately.

Some impromptu menu suggestions include:

- Prepare a favorite casserole. Wrap it well and keep it frozen. Keep on hand a packaged potato or rice side dish and a frozen vegetable. Dinner rolls stored in the freezer come in handy, too. You can now put a meal together. Fruit or berries served over frozen yogurt or ice cream would be a hit for dessert.
- Boboli bread makes excellent pizza. You can make a quick and easy gourmet pizza sauce in minutes by combining spaghetti or pizza sauce with sautéed onion and mushrooms. Sprinkle on some oregano and top with grated cheese.
- Several grocery chains carry stuffed pasta shells. Take as many as you wish from the zippered plastic bag. Place in a sprayed casserole. Top with a prepared spaghetti sauce and

grated cheese. Green peas and seasoned French bread complete the meal.

Quick Refreshments

In addition to one complete meal, every home should have some type of quick-fix refreshments on hand. Here are some ideas:

- A special flavor of herbal tea. Serve in china cups and saucers with linen or decorator paper napkins.
- Heart-shaped crackers and a cheese you particularly enjoy would also be nice with something to drink.
- Packaged or home-baked cookies can be tucked away in the freezer—just in case. One idea is to freeze chocolate chip cookie dough in balls. When company pops in, pull them out of the freezer and bake. You'll have a delicious snack in minutes, and the house will smell wonderfully good.

Pay attention to every detail.

- Something special to drink is nice. My friend Dee serves mint-flavored lemonade. It is her special recipe, and you can always expect it in the summer when you visit. During winter months she keeps wassail ready at all times. I serve a hot tea called orange tea that even tea haters seem to enjoy. Also, I keep on hand my favorite Sundance Raspberry Sparkler for those who prefer something cold to drink.

It doesn't matter so much what it is that you keep on hand as long as you are prepared with something for that unexpected moment when somebody might stop by. It will give you a feeling of confidence to have something tucked away . . . just in case.

Quick Fixes for the Unprepared Home

What can you do besides scream (which isn't too productive) when you have only 10 minutes advance notice that company is coming? Each of us might handle this dilemma differently, but here is what I would do.

- Spend the first five minutes picking up. If you follow your personal daily plan, you shouldn't have that much picking up to do. Remember that people don't notice dust and dirt as much as they notice clutter. Get order at least in the area where you will entertain your guests.
- Spend the next three minutes taking care of special touches.
- Get the smell of potpourri wafting through the house.
- Light a fire in the fireplace if the season allows.
- Softly play recorded instrumental music.
- Light several candles.
- Turn the lights down low!
- Spend the last two minutes on yourself. Change into something presentable, run a comb through your hair, and dab on a little perfume. And smile.

But please, don't apologize. On a scale of 1 to 10, I try to maintain my home at about a 7 or 8 on any given day. I also keep things "picked up" to preserve the appearance of order. But if things are not spotless and perfect, I will not draw attention to the fact by saying, "My house is a mess, blah, blah, blah." That does not make guests feel welcome. If anything, they will feel that they must now apologize for stopping by.

Your unexpected guests have come to see you, not your house. Graciously welcome them and help them to feel comfortable. Consider it an honor to be visited unannounced even though you might prefer some advance notice!

Easy Entertaining

Entertaining, for the most part, costs money, requires time, and calls for planning. It will always take more effort than staying home alone and not inviting others over. But you won't have many friends that way, nor will you be following the biblical injunction to practice hospitality. Although entertaining is work, there are ways of making it easier. Here are some ideas:

- Invite people over for dessert only. Ask guests to join you for it and an evening of fun. Specify clearly that you are serving only dessert so they can eat their meal before they arrive.
- Order in take-out food. You prepare the table and dessert. Chinese food is a good choice here. It costs more to entertain this way, but is easy.
- Invite friends for an open house. This calls for a buffet meal or a multitude of snacks, but leaves you free to circulate. It also allows you to entertain a larger group than you could at one sit-down meal. Have friends drop in between specified hours.
- Plan a Can-You-Top-This Party. For this event you prepare baked potatoes and guests bring their favorite potato topping. You supply tossed salad, bread, and dessert.
- A Progressive Dinner. At a progressive dinner a group visits three or possibly four homes. At each one they eat a portion. For several years we did this at Christmas with friends. At the first home we enjoyed soup, salad, and bread. At my home we had the entrée and veggies. The evening ended at the third home with dessert and a hot drink. We had a wonderful meal and enjoyed seeing three homes decorated for Christmas.

> *Nothing will ever be attempted if all possible objections must be overcome first.*

- A Salad Supper. Invite guests to bring their favorite salad. Specify if you want a pasta, potato, jello, or tossed salad. You prepare bread, drink, and dessert. Perfect for summer entertaining.
- Take guests out to eat. If you are not comfortable with all the preparation or the cooking, have friends out to eat at your favorite restaurant. We were fortunate enough last month to have friends invite us to enjoy some excellent

Chinese food with them. After a wonderful dinner together we joined our host couple at their home for dessert and an evening of great conversation.

- A Soup Supper. Inviting friends over to enjoy a hearty soup supper is an easy and economical way to entertain. If you are a little more adventuresome, you can put a twist on this and ask each guest to bring a portion of the ingredients, which they will prepare in your kitchen—built-in entertainment as everyone gets involved in chopping, grating, and mixing. This would be great for a winter party.
- Potluck it. This truly is the best way of entertaining frequently. It is especially good to use with a group of friends, since they understand that they will share in the preparation. Just remember that every time you entertain your friends, you will also invite someone outside your circle to join you. That's the bottom line!

Do things with style. Develop your own personal entertaining style and then do things with flair. If you have the country look, use an old quilt for a tablecloth. Wear a long hostess gown—even if it is old—if you like it and it makes you feel good. God created in you a very unique personality with individuality, style, and creativity. Don't be afraid to develop it and use it to its full potential even if it is a little unconventional.

Some of us will be more formal, some more casual, some like country crafts, some like sleek and shiny contemporary things. For instance, now that my children are gone from home I use place mats with crystal goblets and candlelight almost every day, just for Harry and me. This is what makes me feel good for where I am today. It's my personal style and doesn't have to be yours. Whatever your likes, develop them, but do it with delight, remembering to thank our Creator-God for giving you the talents and abilities He has for service to others.

Entertaining may not be easy, but it can be made easier. We

each have to determine what is important in our lives. God has given each of us just so much time. If the Lord has called us to practice hospitality, we then must be willing to adjust to our own limitations and learn every possible shortcut so we can follow His plan more closely.

---

* Several ideas in this chapter are adapted from Mains, pp. 155-161.

Setting a pretty table is not a complicated task once you understand certain principles.

10

SETTING
PRETTY

ttractive table settings add to the social atmosphere you are attempting to create and have a psychological effect on the satisfaction your guests derive from the food and the occasion. Table settings are only one phase of entertaining, but they can be the most attractive part of the occasion and provide a picture-perfect background for the meal.*

Table settings must suit your menu, type of food served, the dining area, as well as the occasion, the people you are serving, and your own artistic abilities. Setting a pretty table is not a complicated task once you understand certain principles. The key to improving your skill is with daily practice. Then when serving company meals, you will handle it with ease.

Three things determine the success of your table settings: (1) the food served; (2) the general decor of your home; and (3) personal flair.

When selecting suitable table settings, first consider the occasion. For example, a Fourth of July family picnic is better served on the patio than as a formal sit-down dinner in the dining room. In addition, also look at the type of food served. Pizza goes better on bright-colored stoneware, paper, or plastic goods. Fine china is best reserved for special occasions.

Table settings, generally speaking, should reflect the decor of the home. If you have French provincial furniture with curved legs, white brocade sofas, crystal chandeliers, and an abundance of mirrors, obviously a Mexican table setting with heavy pottery and piñatas would clash. A more formal setting with fine china and crystal would be in better taste.

My style is a constant search for simplicity, elegance, and quality.
KARL SPRINGER

Sometimes, however, a table setting totally different from the decor can bring real interest to the occasion. But the change should be striking, not shocking. Make your meal memorable in a positive way.

Some friends and I are still chuckling over a certain birthday party. Harry and I and another couple traveled more than an hour to attend a fortieth birthday party scheduled to begin at 6:00 p.m. Although it was not specified on the invitation, we assumed it was a dinner invitation, therefore none of us ate before we left, anticipating food as well as the traditional birthday cake. The food amounted to little more than popcorn and fresh oranges. Eventually a birthday cake appeared, still in a brown Pyrex baking dish—with chocolate frosting oozing over the sides of the dish. The men were starving, and we left early so that we could get something to eat at the nearest restaurant.

Table Setting Types

Table settings fall into three main categories: traditional or formal, contemporary, and country or informal. Use whatever suits your personality, your home, and your lifestyle.

Traditional

The traditional table setting is more formal, and each piece is usually highly detailed. Plates would be of fine china and scrolled with borders and patterns. Sometimes such plates will be ornate, hand-painted, or edged with gold or silver. Glassware that would best complement this formal look is tall and stately crystal, some-times finely etched and trimmed in gold.

Flatware may be of a simple pattern or it may be richly deco-rated from the Baroque period. If you are fortunate enough to have sterling silver flatware, here is the opportunity to show it off to its very best with such dishes. Tall candles in crystal candleholders or a silver candelabra would be good choices for this formal scene.

The traditional setting calls for the look of luxury in table linens as well—damask, embroidered linen, Battenberg lace, or lace in white or off-white would be excellent choices. To be served at such a table is truly an elegant and unforgettable dining experience. It can also be a highly romantic occasion that makes it a memorable choice for an anniversary or Valentine's day dinner for the love of your life.

Contemporary

Contemporary plates are often sleek and smooth. Most fre-quently they sport high-gloss glazes in black and white or bold col-ors, sometimes highlighted with an accent color. The clean lines give this style a dramatic effect.

I have a set of contemporary plates in a brilliant red. When I first tell people in the Creative Hospitality Seminar that I will demonstrate what one can do with red plates, they appear dubious. But after the demonstration they are usually eager to buy red plates too. I use my red plates on white Battenberg lace on Valentine's Day; on my blue place mats with flag napkins for the Fourth of July; on a floral print for more formal occasions; on hunter green place mats for Christmas; and with a Raggedy Ann and Andy col-lection for a children's party.

Glassware to complement the contemporary can be heavy and chunky, or tall and sleek. My mother gave me a set of Franciscan sunflower earthenware and a set of purple Franciscan goblets. The chunky appearance and size, as well as the color and weight, all complement other pieces.

Table linens should also follow the contemporary look and could be geometric designs, brilliant prints, or bright solids. The contemporary table setting produces a dramatic and striking effect.

Informal, or Country

One can define a country table setting as informal dinnerware of heavy pottery, earthenware, ironstone, and stoneware. I have the country look in my kitchen and family room. My everyday dishes, stoneware by Heartland, feature a country setting with houses and sheep. I use this set daily on a variety of place mats and tablecloths to change the mood and color as well as to suit the season and occasion.

You can also use country dishes to serve more informal company meals at the dining room table. From purchased blue plaid cotton fabric I made a tablecloth to complement the dishes.

> *Be faithful to your own taste, because nothing you really like is ever out of style.*
> BILLY BALDWIN

Heavy, short-stemmed goblets suit the country look, as does milk glass. Rough-weave cloths and place mats, and the hand-printed look, also coordinate well with heavy dining pieces. Formal linens and fragile goblets would not look right. Baskets, pewter, copper, and brass also complement the country look nicely.

You can use country accessories from your home on the table. The endless variety of homemade crafts and inexpensive pieces are fun to work with. Since I have a collection of teddy bears, I sometimes arrange them in a basket as a centerpiece and play "The Teddy Bears' Picnic" for background music. I also use such items as wooden spools (for candleholders), Raggedy Ann dolls, hand-made bunnies, etc. The country motif can be every bit as attractive as a formal or a contemporary one.

How the table looks helps shape the atmosphere you are attempting to create. If you have inherited a set of Bavarian china, with crystal and silver to go with it, by all means use it—not to impress others, but to serve them and help to create an atmosphere that says to your guests, "You are special." The very fact that you have these things is reason enough to entertain.

I have china and crystal that I got right off Hoo Hoo's table. And if you don't know who Hoo Hoo is, please go back and read chapter 1. When I use them a host of memories floods over me. In my mind's eye I see myself as a child watching Hoo Hoo through the swinging door that divided the dining area from the kitchen as she graciously presided over her table set with those same beautiful dishes. I see my mother in a black uniform with sheer white apron quickly responding to Hoo Hoo's directions. Now those dishes grace my table. I feel greatly privileged to have had them passed on to me. The hand-painted Coalport from England must be hand washed, but I receive so much joy from using them that I don't mind the added task after the meal.

On the other hand, you don't have to have imported heirloom china to set a pretty table anymore. You can attractively set it with pottery, ironware, and enamelware. Rather than waiting until you have something more elaborate to invite people over, simply use creatively what you presently own. Capitalize on the informal nature of your everyday dishes, for example. Add a colorful tablecloth, a napkin, or a place mat in a contrasting color along with a breadbasket centerpiece, and you've got it.

Don't worry if your set of dishes has pieces missing. Some of the best-dressed tables (like Martha Stewart and elite restaurants) mix and match. You can produce a dramatic effect by alternating dinner plates, one with a pattern and one plain. Let's say, for example, that you have inherited four Blue Willow plates from your grandmother, and can use them only when entertaining four. However, you can extend their use by purchasing four plain white plates and alternating Blue Willow and white. Soup bowls, salad plates, or napkins in a coordinating blue or white could tie it all together.

If you can afford only one set of dishes, make them pure white. You can do more with a white plate than any other. In my hospitality seminar I show how to use a white plate on a white-and-yellow place mat with a white basket of sunflowers; with the rose-patterned reversible place mats; or for fall with a terra-cotta place mat and terra-cotta soup bowl. White plates are the most versatile and practical dishes you can have.

The principle of mixing and matching works with any type of dishes. But colors should blend and pieces should be similar in formality. You wouldn't blend enamel dishes with fine china even if the colors did work together.

Pretty Perky Table Toppers

Table linens are now available in every style, color, and size—from lace to damask. In addition to linen and cotton cloths, plastic cloths are available that can appear unbelievably elegant. They come in attractive colors and styles—even to authentic-appearing Battenberg lace and voile finishes.

Tablecloths are also easy to make from purchased fabrics. Even clumsy seamstresses can usually handle four straight hems cut to fit a table. Another idea is to purchase sheets and hem them to fit. They make pretty but practical table coverings.

My taste is the sum total of all I've ever seen or learned in life.

When purchasing or making tablecloths, plan for a six- to eight-inch drop on each side. It is possible to get by with less, but your table will look better when you have a longer drop.

Generally speaking, tablecloths have two advantages over place mats—you can put more on your table without giving a cluttered appearance, and protector pads under a cloth act as both a silencer and protection from spills and heat.

Although attractive tablecloths are available in a wide selection of colors, fabrics, and styles, you don't have to limit table settings to what you see in stores. Here are some ideas to spark your ingenuity.

- A Battenberg or cutwork lace cloth is a real asset for any formal table setting. Many people avoid Battenberg lace because of the required laundering and ironing. But you can easily solve the problem by using clear plastic over the Battenberg lace. I struggled with this idea for some time before actually trying it, as I didn't know how guests would react. They have responded positively—in fact, I've found many of the people I've entertained have invested in clear plastic too. It is available in three weights (I use the lightweight) from hardware and fabric stores.

- Lace cloths can be used over a wood table or placed over a solid colored cloth for a special effect.

- Sheets in solids and prints make delightful table coverings. After cutting your sheet to size use scraps as bows to accent a centerpiece or as a square to tuck in a breadbasket or for napkins.

- A piece of corduroy in an earth tone provides a textured look for a fall table. Combine with leaves, fruits, and vegetable centerpiece.

- A piece of indoor/outdoor green turf provides a sporting look to a buffet table set for television sports fans.

- An antique red-and-white quilt makes a perfect background for a Fourth of July picnic. Add blue place mats or a lightweight clear plastic to protect the quilt.

- A colorful beach towel makes a perfect table covering for a summer picnic indoors or out-of-doors.

- A floral shawl makes a striking table decoration for an ethnic meal. After returning from Russia, I used a colorful babushka as a table covering and displayed matreshka dolls and a miniature St. Basil's as the centerpiece.

Table Mats

Table mats in various colors, styles, and textures complement your dishes and add pizzazz to a table. They should also harmonize with the room. For instance, I purchased a print with pink roses on a blue background and a coordinating striped print and made my own striking reversible place mats. Napkins are also of the stripes. These color coordinates present a stunning effect.

- Collect a wardrobe of mats and alternate them around a table for an interesting effect.
- Square dinner napkins placed diagonally in front of each diner can serve as place mats. They can also hide stains.
- Lacy paper doilies make elegant place mats, especially effective for a valentine's dinner or when serving sandwiches or dessert. Keep a selection of doilies in various sizes on hand at all times to give a special appearance to plates when serving cookies and desserts.
- Your children can make delightful place mats from cardboard, cork, or poster board. Colorful designs and borders add special touches. Children also enjoy decorating fabrics with fabric paints or glue-on designs.
- For large gatherings, design your own place mats. When our son-in-law graduated from medical school, his family planned a party in his honor. Carlene drew a doctor's jacket and stethoscope on art paper with Brian's name on the pocket. Each mat was then colored with felt pens and laminated with clear plastic. A centerpiece with flowers and a stethoscope and other medical instruments took center stage. The place mat was a clever and economical keepsake for each guest.
- Clear glass panels can be laid over fall leaves or pressed flowers. You can arrange them directly on top of the table or on a cloth. Cover the edges of the panes with colorful tape to prevent cuts, or have your glass cutter polish them smooth.
- Large ceramic tiles make stunning individual place mats.

- You can achieve a layered look by using one longer cloth topped by another shorter cloth placed diagonally. Accent this with coordinating place mats or napkins.
- Use table runners instead of place mats. Cross two runners to seat four at a square table or three runners spaced evenly around a round table to seat six. Use your imagination to create some unusual effects.
- By putting clear plastic over most place mats, you can use them with children and still protect the mats from spills.

Glassware

While formal gatherings require clear glass goblets in a traditional shape, for informal dinners almost anything goes—even jelly glasses. I found a set of jelly glasses with handles that I use when setting a country look. Colorful glassware from Mexico, a collection of unmatched goblets, or ordinary short, straight-sided glasses can create pleasing or even dramatic effects.

Flatware

Most homes take flatware on the table for granted—except mine. One of my favorite parties is one in which I sit the guests at the table with nothing before them but a menu! It lists four courses, and each guest orders for all four courses at the beginning of the meal. What you order is what you get. If you don't order silverware until the last

The dining table is the last retreat of the old values and more human scale of the past.
PATRICK DUNNE

course, you don't get it until then. The menu is somewhat scrambled, of course. It is a hilarious evening with built-in entertainment.

In a dining room drawer I store a set of sterling silver flatware. It truly is lovely on a formal table with a floral centerpiece and tall candles. But few occasions call for it anymore—at least for my lifestyle. The more popular way of entertaining today is with one of the popular stainless steel patterns available in a broad range of both simple and elegant patterns.

Stainless steel eliminates all the polishing required in yesteryear's entertaining. And you can pop stainless steel into the dishwasher for easy washing. It is every bit as shiny as sterling and comes in a vast assortment of styles and patterns for individual tastes.

Tips for creative use of flatware:

- Most of the time you will probably use matching flatware. But you might also like to pick up knives, forks, and spoons at garage sales or outlet centers and build a collection of unmatched but harmonizing flatware to make an interesting statement at your table.
- Sets of "service for one" in several harmonizing patterns can make a delightful change.
- Inexpensive flatware with colored plastic handles adds color and style to a table. I have a set in red that I can use with my red plates on Valentine's Day, the Fourth of July, Christmas, and a host of other occasions. I also have service for two in blue for "picnic dates" with Harry.
- Collect specialized serving pieces of various sizes and shapes. I have inherited several unique and beautiful serving spoons that are conversation pieces which add a special touch to my table.

Napkins—Not in the Usual Fold

The napkin apparently dates back to the days of nobility and wealth. The rich adorned their dining tables with expensive linens and silk draperies. The cloths were set diagonally over long tables with a point centered in front of each diner. It seems, however, that the diners' table manners did not match the ornate settings. It was common practice for people to wipe greasy hands on their equally ornate clothing.

Someone with a most creative mind thought of taking the corner that hung in front of each diner and tucking it under the chin to form a swinging bib and catch food spills. After the meal diners would wipe their hands and mop up spills with the corner in front of them!

History has failed to record the inventor of the first napkin. But by the fifteenth century it had become fashionable to tie the napkin around the neck. This practice protected the ruffles, laces, and velvet worn by both sexes of the era.

The napkin has remained with us through the years and progressed in use, color, and style. Today it plays a double role, protecting clothing and assisting with the presentation of the food.

Most entertaining calls for cloth napkins. For more informal dining you can combine quality paper napkins with a cloth table covering. Whatever the material, you can fold and place them under the fork on the left, tuck them creatively into a goblet when you need a splash of color, or slip them through a napkin ring and lay them across or above the plate. The napkin has become an integral part of all well-set tables.

Napkins can either match the tablecloth or be of a contrasting or coordinating color. Innovative napkin arrangements help create an ambiance that makes the difference between another ho-hum meal and a truly memorable experience. Today colored napkins can, in some cases, replace floral arrangements, especially at luncheons and less formal occasions.

> *A thing of beauty is a joy forever.*
> JOHN KEATS

Paper napkins are available in all colors, patterns, and styles, and are acceptable for family gatherings, potluck dinners, large crowds, picnics, and more informal events.

Folding napkins into interesting shapes can surprise and delight guests. My three favorite ways of presenting the napkin are (1) folded and placed under the fork, (2) gathered into a napkin ring and placed in the center of the plate, and (3) tucked into the goblet. Any napkin folding book can provide more intricate folds.

Some interesting ways of presenting the napkin follow:

- Take two napkins of contrasting color and tuck them into the goblet or through a napkin ring.
- From purchased eyelet make a square. Place it over any napkin of your choice and present it either in the goblet or in a napkin ring. This gives a stunning effect, especially if you have a matching eyelet tablecloth placed over the same fabric.
- Colorful bandannas make napkins for a Western meal and theme. Use blue denim for a tablecloth.
- When serving such foods as corn on the cob or other foods eaten with the fingers, place a packet of premoistened towelettes next to each napkin for your guest's convenience.

Napkin rings can add interest as well as a finishing touch to your table. Following are some special touches that you do with napkin rings:

- For something that says "you are special," tuck a rosebud into each woman's napkin and a carnation into each male guest's napkin.
- For a fall meal tie napkins with raffia.
- Tiny grapevine wreaths make interesting napkin rings for a country look. Decorate with dried flowers.
- French ribbon (ribbon with wire so that it holds its shape) can also tie a napkin. Hunter green ribbon edged with gold on a red napkin would be stunning for a Christmas dinner. Add a gold bell in the center.
- Gold braid tied around a napkin provides an elegant touch to a more formal dinner.
- Tie bows on napkins with yarn ribbon or curling ribbon in a range of colors.
- Purchase napkin rings in wood, ceramic, or metal to complement your table decor.

The Well-set Table

Making your table an attractive place to eat not only involves having the right combination of tablecloths, mats, napkins, china, flatware, etc., but also calls for knowing how to set the table correctly. Learning how to set a table properly is not time-consuming or difficult. A few basic rules and pictures will do it. Yet some people seem unable to handle the basics of table settings.

On one occasion a newly married 19-year-old guest asked if she could help me do anything. The plates were on the table, so I asked if she'd handle the silverware. Her bewildered expression and embarrassed manner told me she didn't know where the silverware went. I led her to the table and obviously gave her her first lesson in table setting! Had no one ever required her to set a table in her 19 years? Had she never gone out to eat and observed even the basic rules of forks to the left of the plate and knife and spoon to the right? Mothers, we've got to do better than this! Children of both sexes need to know how to set a table correctly. Such simple social graces go a long way in all the years to come.

Depending on the style of service, you set the dinner plates in the center of each place setting, or in a stack in front of the person who will be serving for family-style service. To avoid crowding guests, allow 20 to 30 inches for each place setting. Place forks, knives, and spoons in order of use with first items used on the outside. This makes it easier for guests to know which item to choose. Position china, silver, and napkins about one inch from the edge of the table (see figure 1 in Appendix A).

Place forks to the left of the plate. If you serve the salad prior to the main course, put the salad fork on the left of the dinner fork. If the salad accompanies or follows the main course, put the salad fork on either side of the dinner fork. A salad fork is not essential if the salad accompanies the main course.

Knives and spoons go to the right of the plate with the knife closest to the plate and the blade facing the plate. Drawings show how to set the table for each course (see figure 2 in Appendix A).

Drawing 1: The appetizer course shows the napkin, silverware, and glassware for the rest of the meal.

Drawing 2: The soup course. Provide a soup spoon. Place bowl on an underliner plate. Usually you would not have both an appetizer and a soup course, but one or the other. An informal dinner often omits both.

Cultivate the habit of attention at home.

Drawing 3: The main course. Dinner plate, salad plate (optional), bread-and-butter plate and knife (optional), dinner fork, salad fork (optional), knife and spoon. Provide a glass for beverage.

When you have a bread-and-butter plate, place it above the forks, with the bread-and-butter knife straight across the top of the plate. (This plate is used for more formal dinners only and may be omitted if table space is limited.)

The salad plate may appear in several positions. When you do not use a bread-and-butter plate, place the salad plate at the tip of the forks. When you do have a bread-and-butter plate, position the salad plate to the left and below the bread and butter plate.

The napkin rests on the left of the forks with the open corners at the lower right. If you use both salad and bread-and-butter plates, place the napkin on the dinner plate. When you want a fancy fold, you can place the napkin almost anywhere as long as you do it tastefully.

The water glass or goblet belongs at the tip of the knife.

Drawing 4: The dessert course. Dessert is usually served from the kitchen with the necessary silverware. A hot beverage may accompany the dessert at the table or come later in the evening.

Remember, entertaining nowadays has few absolutes to follow. To a large extent you can do as you please (within limits). Whether it works for you is the important thing, and that you know what you plan to do.

The general rules for etiquette and common sense still apply in more uncommon situations. Think through the event and plan in advance. Keep the comfort of guests paramount in your mind.

If you make a few mistakes along the way, you will only be like the rest of us.

Recently I traveled to Poland to teach a Compleat Marriage and Courtship Seminar to a church in Poznan. Each evening following the seminar, the local elder invited me to his home located in the large building that housed the church and several apartments. Around the table sat my sister, Ginger, who accompanied me on the trip, my translator, Pastor Roman Chalupka, two men who made up a local TV crew, and the host and his wife. It was an interesting mix of people. Some spoke only English (Ginger and I), one knew seven languages (my translator), some spoke limited English (such as my host), and one spoke no English at all (my hostess).

The light meal was always prettily set. Somehow I had assumed that in Poland people didn't worry about "setting pretty." Lovely dishes graced the table, napkins had been creased into interesting folds, and sometimes fresh flowers served as decorations (don't ask me how they got Antherium in Poland!).

The conversation was always stimulating—sometimes so much so that translation would be forgotten, much to the consternation of those not understanding whatever language was being used at the moment. At the end of nine evenings with these special people, around their table (a round table, mind you), we found our hearts bound together in a way that could not have happened outside of "breaking bread" to-gether. Without a translator I couldn't have even thanked the hostess for all her efforts since she spoke not a word of English. Fortunately, I had learned one Polish word—*Jenkuya* (thank you).

On my last evening after we had all debriefed about the meet-ing, someone asked what I would remember from Poland. Without hesitation I told them it would be the friendships established around the table. My fondest memories are of those people who so gra-ciously shared their meager food rations with me, and who refused to accept any money because it was their gift to me and their church. In spite of their limited English they had warmly welcomed me to their table.

What this Polish family did for me, you can do for someone else. There is someone out there who is lonely and discouraged, someone who needs an invitation to your table. Open your heart and your home to become the encourager God wants you to be.

---

*The table-setting suggestions are from several sources, including the author and Hospitality seminars. Other ideas are adapted from Collier.

A beautiful centerpiece
is the center of attention when entertaining guests.

11

CENTERPIECES

he centerpiece of yesterday used to mean a formal floral arrangement. Today it includes table decorations of all kinds, including artificial flowers, live plants, fruits and vegetables, candles, knickknacks from around the house, or anything interesting used to complete a theme.

In today's more relaxed style of entertaining a large imposing floral arrangement, especially when plunked dead center on the table and flanked by tall taper candles on either side, reeks of formality. It almost says out loud, "Ladies and gentlemen, you are in for a most serious evening." Leave such formality and seriousness to the president and government heads. Remember, your goal is to create an atmosphere of warmth and friendship.

A beautiful centerpiece is the center of attention when entertaining guests. But don't wait till you are entertaining to have centerpieces. Both the kitchen and dining table should always have them. It's fun to change them with the season. As I write, it is fall and Thanksgiving is around the corner. The dining table has a wooden bowl filled with fruit—apples, oranges, lemons, persimmons, pomegranates, grapes, and small gourds. This spills out onto colorful fall leaves, a miniature pumpkin, and two Pilgrims.

On the kitchen table I have my "instant arrangement." The instant arrangement is for those who love fresh flowers but don't have time or don't know how to arrange flowers. Here's the secret.

Creating a beautiful home is a high artistic achievement; enjoying it is the art of living.

Purchase two four-inch pots of mums (or any blooming flowers). Set them side by side in a basket. Stick some sprigs of ivy into the dirt or add a tiny pot of ivy. Cover the tops with moss so you can't see the pots. Presto—instant arrangement! You will really wow your friends with your new talent. An arrangement adorns my kitchen table during most seasons. Come spring it will contain primroses.

When planning a centerpiece, do remember that it must be low enough so that it does not obstruct vision and conversation. Any centerpiece that is tall enough to make family or guests lean to one side or the other in order to see those across the table is too high. Worse yet would be one that obstructed the view entirely.

The key to creating interesting centerpieces is to improvise, improvise, improvise. It also helps to have available an interesting assortment of unusual containers to hold your centerpiece. Some things that you can use are baskets, toy trucks, teapots, antique coffeepots, pitchers, bowls, vases, old liquor bottles, jars, musical instruments, dolls, and teddy bears.

Centerpiece Ideas

Although it would be impossible to give an exhaustive list of ideas, here are a few to prime the pump and help you recognize what you might have under your own roof:*

- Arrange fresh fruits and/or vegetables in a wooden bowl or basket to make a delightful and edible centerpiece. Since it is currently lemon season in California, I have a mound of lemons arranged on a plain white plate. I tucked a few lemon leaves in here and there for greenery. It is simple but striking on a Battenberg lace cloth.

- Try shiny red and/or green apples in a rough basket at Christmas. Tuck in sprigs of holly for contrast. Add a plaid bow in Christmas colors for a country holiday look.

- White daisies with ivy in an old copper teakettle make a perky and pretty centerpiece.

- Into five or six old canning jars stuff some buttercups, daisies, or Queen Anne's lace. Accent the grouping with two or three fresh lemons on the table next to the jars.

- Get out your punch bowl and collect an assortment of tall flowers such as three gladiolus sprays, four carnations, and five irises. Bind all stems together with florist wire. Stand the bound stems in a multipronged metal flower stand in the center of the punch bowl. Partially fill with water. Float additional blossoms in the pool of water. For additional pizzazz, place a punch cup filled with a mini bouquet at each place setting around the table.

- Cluster a collection of graceful vases on a mirror at the center of the table. Place one delicate long-stemmed flower in each vase along with some trailing ivy for a beautiful effect. Ivy can be curved into any shape you wish with floral wire.

- Fresh herbs make a delightful addition to centerpieces. Nosegays of parsley and mint look attractive in demitasse or egg cups, and finger bowls will serve to hold bouquets of pansies or violets. One mini arrangement per place setting is ideal.

- Fill a large wooden salad bowl with red apples, pinecones, and clusters of purple grapes. Accent with tall red or purple candles arranged around the bowl.

- Place a bunch of black-eyed Susans in a white pitcher and set on a white dinner plate in the center of the table. Surround the pitcher with lemons and sprigs of mint for added color and aroma.

- Place mini-bouquets of wildflowers, grasses, and herbs in cups and set one at each place setting.
- Put a potted small-leafed ivy in the center of a basket with branches trailing over the edges. Surround the ivy with polished red and green apples, small clusters of grapes, and whole walnuts. Simple and spectacular.
- Colorful ribbon by the bolt adds a festive accent to a table centerpiece. Around a centerpiece of shiny red Christmas ornaments I wind yards and yards of two-inch plain Christmas ribbon, allowing it to fall as it may off the bolt to either side on top of greenery. To the generous coils of ribbon I add garlands of metallic stars. Several tall candles along with clear Christmas lights increase the drama.
- Satiny pastel ribbons can also be used on a table anchored in the center under the centerpiece. Allow the curls to drape over the sides of the table. This is particularly effective for birthday parties. Coordinate the colors—purple with hot pink would be striking. Add balloons in the same shades, and your guest of honor will love it.

The ability to simplify means to eliminate the unnecessary so that the necessary may speak.
HANS HOFMANN

- For a child's party, use solid white or pastel vinyl cloth. Write each guest's name on the table above the plate in washable felt tip markers. Then provide markers for the children to draw pictures or write messages on the cloth. Each child could also design his or her own place mat for the table. Colorful face cloths make practical and pretty napkins.
- For an original fall centerpiece, collect colored leaves and press them between sheets of waxed paper. This makes the leaves shiny. Scatter them down the center of the table. Votive candles would look nice placed randomly throughout the leaves. Excellent project to do with children.

- Treasured objects from around your home can create original centerpieces: a grouping of musical instruments, old toy banks or cars, a teapot, or an antique lace runner made by your grandmother produce unique table arrangements. One interesting accessory from the collection beside each place setting makes an interesting statement and will spark excellent table conversation.
- Place a few blossoms in tiny egg cups and use at each place setting. This is a delightful way of using egg cups that might otherwise remain stored in a cupboard forever.
- A basket of juicy oranges or tangerines adds warmth and charm to a table. Sprays of evergreens give the final touch.
- Line a basket with red and orange tissue paper and fill with a mound of rosy peaches.
- Invert a straw hat and fill the cavity with a potted plant.
- Fill an enameled colander with polished red and green apples or any fruit. Surround it with white votive candles.
- Line a pretty sewing basket with aluminum foil. Fill with nectarines, oranges, purple plums, and clusters of green grapes.
- Heap a glass bowl with apples, oranges, dates, dried figs, and unshelled walnuts and almonds. Hang nutcrackers around the edge of the bowl.

_____

*Ideas adapted from several sources, including Collier.

An old saying states, "Food should feed the eyes first."

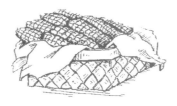

FOOD PRESENTATION ART

*A*n old saying states, "Food should feed the eyes first." Yes, the need for nourishment and the desire for pleasure are sensations that we should combine. When we think of eating, we think about all the pleasant sensations that accompany it—taste, aroma, color, and texture. When we harmoniously join these elements with good conversation and hospitality, dining becomes more than providing needed nourishment.

The way we present food to family and guests expresses many aspects of our lives—lifestyle, culture, and family traditions. By the manner in which we serve food we can either show love or withhold it.

Food satisfies our senses of taste, smell, sight, touch, and comfort. When we serve it pleasantly, it will nourish our souls as well as our bodies.

We can use food to meet a number of different needs once we understand this fact. The key to achieving the maximum benefits from food lies in thoughtful presentation of each meal. It takes only a little creativity and a little caring. The way you serve food expresses who and what you are and what you think of yourself. It will either delight or dampen a guest's expectation. An attractive presentation of food can whet the appetite and put your visitors in an expectant and receptive mood. Although an important part of any meal, it is *not* complicated.

Recently in a bookstore I bumped into a friend I hadn't seen for a while. As she ranted on about her stressed life I knew I had a candidate for my next Personalized Home Organization Seminar. I shared some of the topics it covered with her. When I got to "Menu Planning Made Easy," she shrieked, "I am so exhausted by the time I get home after a long day that I don't care what kind of slop I throw in the kids' mouths." Without actually telling me, she was saying volumes about herself, her values, and how she functions in her home.

It's true that most of us live hectic lives and don't have as much time to devote to food presentation as did people of yesteryear. But that's exactly why we need a reminder about serving our meals creatively to the ones we love. We also need some speedy methods of doing it.

The way we present food, however, goes beyond decorating a platter. Color, texture, flavor combinations, quantity and arrangement of food, serving containers, centerpieces, and lighting are all part of making eating pleasurable. When we have carefully considered these factors and when we have combined casualness with a touch of originality and creativity, then food presentation becomes a form of art.

The art of serving food that is both tasty and aesthetically attractive makes cooking pleasurable. You will receive some enjoyment just from menu planning, shopping, chopping, simmering, and beating. But it really is the sharing of your labors with others that makes your efforts worthwhile. However, if you attempt more than you can handle comfortably, stressing yourself unduly during the preparation, you will be exhausted and get discouraged. It is far better to prepare a simple meal than to attempt a complicated menu that will be hard on your nerves.*

Taste

Taste, more than any of our other senses, involves personal choice. A flavor that appeals to one person, another will dislike. Individual taste preferences are difficult to predict. It is next to impossible, then, for any one cook to please everyone all the time. A safe rule of thumb when cooking for guests with unknown personal taste preferences is to go easy on the seasonings. This in no way implies that you must cook bland meals, but it is safer to stick with more common foods enjoyed by most people rather than preparing a more exotic menu with rare spices and herbs.

Within the family we become familiar with personal preferences and work around them. Our offspring weren't finicky, picky eaters. But even so, Rodney can't handle pears, or Mark onions, or Carlene breakfast. Harry will eat almost anything I put before him—but please, no tomato soup! I am not fond of cottage cheese. Even those with good appetites have individualistic taste preferences. Over a period of time, however, we can put together several guest menus that seem to please most of our guests most of the time.

Aroma

The tempting aroma of food often reaches our guests long before they are seated at the table. The beckoning whiff of a tasty casserole or the haunting scent of a pot simmering on the stove is enough to fill people with keen anticipation.

The tantalizing smell of homemade bread or cookies baking can elicit fond memories and create an irresistible surge of delight. A wise cook understands what aroma can do and will use it to her advantage.

Here are a few tips to help you use aroma effectively:

- Gently sautéing an onion not only gives off a pleasing aroma but will add flavor to the pan juices. (It also works wonders when you are behind schedule and your family wants to eat *now!* Sauté an onion while you are getting the table set and everyone will wait more patiently because of the aroma.)

- Experiment with herbs, spices, citrus peelings, and garlic to heighten cooking aromas.
- Use preheated, *covered* serving dishes. They will keep your food warm but will also release a heavenly aroma when you raise the lid.
- Caution: Strongly scented perfumes, scented candles, simmering pot potpourri, and fuel for oil lamps may sometimes overpower your cooking aromas. Use them all wisely.

Color

When presenting food, color is the most exciting component you can use to stimulate the senses. Colorful food is both appetizing and festive. From the vivid red of a sweet bell pepper to the subtle beige of a mushroom, color delights the eyes.

As you plan your menu, be attentive to the rainbow of colors God has provided. A main dish can be attractively complemented by colorful vegetables steamed properly to retain their natural color and crunch. Here are some colorful suggestions designed to spark ideas in your mind:

- Combine two or more vegetables for color impact. For example: peas and sliced rounds of carrots; steamed carrot sticks with green beans; broccoli and cauliflower florets; a head of cauliflower steamed and served on a platter surrounded with green peas; green peas with a red pimento or with sliced mushrooms.
- Serve golden corn on the cob in a wicker basket lined with a blue-and-white checked linen towel.
- When serving cauliflower on white dishes, use leaves of raw spinach as a colorful bed for the florets. Sprinkle with grated lemon rind to enhance the color and aroma.
- Serve coleslaw in a glass bowl lined with ruffled cabbage leaves. Sprinkle finely grated carrot over for added flavor and eye appeal.

- As you cook cauliflower, add a spoonful of lemon juice to the water to keep the vegetable snowy white.
- When serving vegetable stew with the usual carrots and green beans, heighten the color impact by adding strips of blanched red bell pepper. Serve on bright-red ceramic plates. Striking!
- You can enhance the eye appeal of beets, carrots, or potatoes by fringing the edges of a white serving bowl with springs of parsley or watercress.
- To the whiteness of potato salad add a chopped red apple and serve on ruffled red lettuce.
- To make rice pink, replace half the liquid in the recipe with an equal quantity of tomato juice.
- For intense flavor in your rice as well as a warm color, replace the water in your rice recipe with an equal amount of chick-enlike seasoned liquid.

Nature has provided us with a stunning palette of fruits, vegetables, and herbs that you can use to dress and garnish food. Build on these ideas to create a multitude of new colorful ways to give the food you serve even more eye appeal.

Texture

Texture involves the coarseness or smoothness of food and how it feels in our mouths. Again, personal choice can influence a fondness for texture. Some people prefer vegetarian patties made from chopped nuts because they like the crunchiness. I prefer making patties from ground nuts, as I don't like the crunchiness.

You can alter the texture of most foods by how much cooking time you allow. This is particularly true of vegetables. When cooked to perfection, vegetables can retain their vibrant color and crunch (which is a delight to the palate). But when cooked too long, they can lose their color, get limp, and have less nutritional value.

Some new ways to add variety to texture are:
- Add a diced Delicious apple to potato salad.

- Add a coarsely chopped carrot to peanut butter.
- To veggie burgers add a finely shredded raw potato.

A good combination at any meal is to strive for some chewing, a little mashing, and a bit of crunch. But these are only a few ideas that can make a big difference in food texture.

Serving Food With Style

If I asked you how many serving dishes you had, you would probably mentally begin to count the traditional bowls you ordinarily use. But you probably have dozens of unique pieces you never thought of using as food containers before.

Instead of purchasing new serving dishes, may I suggest that you take a fresh look at what you might already have available. A gold mine of serving pieces may be sitting unused in your cupboards. Let's bring them out to be enjoyed in new and different ways. Who says a cake plate has to be reserved only for cake, or a colander only for rinsing noodles? The innovative ideas here are presented in order to spark ideas in you.

Food Presentation Ideas

One large **glass bowl** can be a tremendous asset for colorful food presentation. Here are some suggested things you can use it for:
- A layered green salad: lay down a bed of shredded lettuce, followed by cherry or chopped tomatoes, garbanzo or red kidney beans, chopped green onions, and alfalfa sprouts.
- A layered fruit salad. Start with marbles of seedless green grapes and top with wedges of nectarines, watermelon, or cantaloupe cubes, purple plum halves, orange sections, and sliced kiwi.
- Potato or macaroni salad.
- Tuck a napkin inside the bowl and fill it with a mound of homemade rolls. Poke bread sticks in between the rolls for added dimension.

Rice bowls, both large and small, have limitless uses in the kitchen as well as on the table. They come in decorative geometric and Oriental patterns that can be fun to mix and match. Try them for serving:

- Grapefruit.
- Condiments such as relish, chutney, jams, or jellies.
- Soup.
- Ice cream, fruit cups, puddings, or other desserts.
- Rice.
- Chili.
- Cereal.
- A do-it-yourself salad bar. Place a large bowl of salad greens in the center of your table. Circle it with rice bowls containing a selection of salad fixings: green onion, garbanzo beans, green peas, bacon bits, sliced beets, cherry tomatoes, or croutons.
- Artichokes. Add a second rice bowl to hold discarded artichoke leaves or a dip for the artichokes.

Cake plate. Besides just holding a cake, you can find many uses for a large round cake plate either with or without a pedestal.

- Pies, tarts, cupcakes, pastries, cheeses, and pizza.
- Centerpieces containing fresh whole pears, peaches, grapes, and bananas can be arranged in a stunning manner. Stud the arrangement with Bing cherries and a few green leaves.
- Present a steaming vegetarian loaf or patties on a pedestal cake plate. Surround it with boiled red potatoes, alternating with broccoli florets.
- Set a round fruitcake on a cake stand and surround it with snips of holiday greenery. Top the fruitcake with candied red and green cherries and pecan halves.
- Arrange two golden Delicious apples and a bunch of seedless green grapes next to a generous wedge of Brie cheese for another natural but beautiful centerpiece.

Coffee and tea pots. In addition to serving hot drinks in them,

consider the following uses for coffee and tea pots:
- Charming dispensers for hot soup. They also make interesting centerpieces into which you can arrange fresh and silk flowers.

Demitasse cups and saucers.
- Fill the cups halfway with crushed ice; use as individual containers for butter curls with the saucer serving as a bread plate.
- Containers for dessert sauces, such as a chocolate or raspberry sauce.
- As a first course, serve your favorite dip in the cup with raw vegetables such as radishes, zucchini slices, and broccoli on the saucer. For a nutritious afternoon snack, stand a few red and green bell pepper strips up in the cup.

Carafes. These gracefully shaped pouring vessels offer many possibilities:
- To hold any chilled drink, milk, or fruit juice.
- As a straw dispenser.
- To hold bread sticks if the carafe has a wide mouth.
- As a vase to hold a bunch of flowers. Tie a pretty bow around it for added flair.

How beautiful a day can be when kindness touches it.

Colander. Some colanders are pretty enough to be brought from behind the scenes to the table. Try them for
- A brunch centerpiece to hold some brown and white cooked eggs.
- A bread basket. Nest a linen napkin in it and pile hot rolls inside.
- Pile individual boxes of cereal in a colander for easy serving for family or company.

Cookie jars. If your cookie jar is heat-resistant, in addition to holding cookies, it could also be used at the table
- To serve stew, hot soup, or even chili.
- As a container for coleslaw.
- As a container for a bunch of white lilacs or some other flowers.

Cutting board. Cutting boards are wooden slabs designed for slicing foods. But you can adapt a cutting board of either a plain or fancy shape for the following purposes:

- To serve bread, cheese, or fruit.
- As a serving bed for steamed corn on the cob after you lay a bed of freshly shucked corn leaves on the board.
- As great trivets for hot foods.

Egg cups. Egg cups offer an ideal way to present individual servings of:

- Margarine or butter
- Vegetable dips
- Salad dressings
- Dessert sauces

Ice buckets. An ice bucket, whether stainless steel, wood, or crystal, offers several possibilities at the table.

- Stand thin loaves of French bread up in an ice bucket. Add a few stalks of sea oats (from a floral center) and a red-and-yellow plaid bow, and you have a very pretty container.
- Line an ice bucket with a striped terry hand towel. Serve ears of corn standing upright.

Pitchers. Pitchers, with their graceful shapes and inviting handle, also make attractive additions to a table.

- Serve orange juice and milk from a pitcher rather than cartons.
- Serve bread sticks in it.
- Use it as a vase for flowers.

Punch bowls. The large punch bowl that you have stored somewhere in your house (I couldn't find mine when I went looking for it last week) has other uses besides punch.

- As a tureen for chilled soups. Serve soup in the matching cups.
- As a salad bowl for a large crowd. The cups can hold dressing.
- Float candles and flowers and use it as a centerpiece. Put a cup with a flower at each place setting.
- As a centerpiece for displaying fresh fruit. Place a generous

layer of ice cubes at the bottom. Top with an arrangement of peaches, nectarines, and plums. Place bouquets of violets in cups to accent the plums.

Soup tureens. Tureens are ordinarily used to serve soup. But this deep bowl can be adapted in other ways.

- For stew or chili.
- Punch.
- Popcorn.
- Spaghetti.
- Tossed salad.
- Fruit compote.
- As a potholder for a potted plant.
- As a vase for an arrangement of daffodils, forsythia, or lilacs.

Sugar bowls and creamers. You can use them individually or together in several ways as containers for

- A dip.
- Parmesan cheese.
- Small flower arrangements.
- Nut dishes.
- Chutney or relish.
- Jam or honey.
- Sour cream in the creamer; chopped chives in the sugar bowl.
- Syrups and sauces.
- Raisins to sprinkle on cereals.

Act as if it were impossible to fail.

Glasses. Glasses, tumblers, and goblets provide many practical ways for serving.

- Fruit cups of berries, melon balls, and sliced peaches.
- Cold puddings.
- Parfaits.
- For a scoop of ice cream with raspberry sauce and garnished with a sprig of mint.
- Gelatin desserts.

- Try serving vegetable juice in a stemmed goblet with a celery swizzle stick for garnish.

Bottles. Instead of throwing all bottles away, save some for your table. Bottles of different shapes make interesting containers once you have soaked the labels off. They can be used as

- Candleholders.
- Water pitchers.
- Vases for long-stemmed flowers. Group several bottles together with one flower in each bottle.
- As a container for serving lemonade, fruit punch, or milk.

---

* Suggestions in this chapter are adapted from Collier.

Toasts can be made with any drink—fruit punch, soda, water, or milk.

TOASTS: REVIVING A GRAND TRADITION

Many Christians have, generally speaking, avoided toasts because traditionally toasting a person has involved doing so with alcohol. But by rejecting them they have tossed out a lovely way of honoring someone simply because of a misconception. Let's take a second look at toasts.

The purpose of a toast is to give honor to someone, to affirm, congratulate, or show respect to anyone who has earned it. Wedding anniversaries, birthdays, a new job, raises, graduations, and retirements are all occasions on which toasts could play an important part in making the event memorable. But you don't have to wait for a momentous happening to honor someone.

Anyone at the gathering can propose a toast, but usually the host initiates it. At weddings the best man proposes a toast, and at wedding anniversaries children propose toasts to their parents. Toasts are better not done on the spur of the moment. If a person is truly going to be honored, the person preparing the toast should have something intelligent to say. Most of us would have trouble giving an extemporaneous accolade. It really needs thoughtful consideration and should be written in advance. At just the right time bring it out and read it if you have not committed it to memory. This is much better than stumbling around for words and in your search for something to say, coming up with something ridiculous, or worse yet, embarrassing.

It is customary that the person proposing the toast stand. In a small group usually nothing more needs to be said than "I would like to propose a toast . . ." in order to gain the group's attention. At a large function such as a reception, the person proposing the toast may tap a piece of flatware against the rim of a glass—*carefully*. It could be disconcerting to break a glass at this point. The person being toasted does not stand or drink with the others when being toasted.

Toasts can be made with any drink—fruit punch, soda, water, or milk. Many fine nonalcoholic drinks have come on the market today that you could use for special occasions. But you do not need a glass to participate. It is perfectly proper just to raise your arm when others do.

At a twenty-fifth wedding anniversary the best man, if present, could propose the toast. It might sound something like this:

"Many of us here tonight remember Jim and Mary's wedding 25 years ago. We wished them future happiness and God's richest blessings then. This has served them well. And now, 25 years later, we are together with Jim and Mary, old friends and new. I am asking that all of you rise with me as we wish Jim and Mary another 25 years of love and happiness."

Notice the toast was simple, direct, and to the point. Toasts should *never* be long, involved, or complicated. It is not the time to tell stories about the couple. The purpose of a toast is to honor, not to make fun of or to ridicule, as funny as a story might be. Keep the toast short, sweet, simple, and highly complimentary.

If it suits the occasion, you might use a biblical toast. Many passages of Scripture lend themselves to toasts and could be an excellent and subtle witness. The one I used to honor my mother on Christmas Eve as the matriarch of the family lent itself well to the occasion:

" 'Lord, . . . You have granted [her] the desire of [her] heart
and have not withheld the request of [her] lips.
You welcomed [her] with rich blessings
and placed a crown of pure gold on [her] head.
[She] asked you for life,
And you gave it to [her]—
length of days forever and ever.
Through the victories you gave,
[her] glory is great;
you have bestowed on [her] splendor and majesty.'
[Psalm 21:1-5, NIV].

"Thank you, Mother, for opening your home to us on this
Christmas Eve. We appreciate you!"

A passage like this would be equally suitable to honor a pastor,
a grandparent, or anyone on his or her retirement.

Till now everyone has remained seated but the one proposing
the toast. Now, after the toast, everyone, except the person being
honored, rises. The person being toasted always remains seated.
Everyone touches glasses or clinks them with those around them. It
is not necessary to clink glasses with everyone present—two or
three persons will suffice.

The clinking of glasses is like saying "Amen." Obviously everyone present cannot speak personally or give a toast, and so those
present are actually doing so by clinking their glasses with others. It
shows a unity of spirit, a oneness among those present to give honor.

Customarily, the person being toasted will respond with a short
speech to thank those involved. My mother on Christmas Eve simply said, *"Skoal! Skoal!"* (Swedish for "to your health").

Emily Post tells the story of a little girl sent to America during
World War II to escape the bombing in London. On the day of her
arrival in America her host family was giving a posh dinner party.
The little girl was a tired and bewildered guest at the fancy dinner

after the long trip. The host, however, rose and offered a toast. "Jennifer, we welcome you to America," he said, "but first I want to propose a toast to His Majesty the king of England." With tears in her eyes, tired little Jennifer stood and lifted her glass of milk with the rest, all the while acting like she had been doing it all her life. In a clear voice she said, "To His Majesty the king." She knew what to do because she had been doing it all her life.*

At our Christmas Eve celebration I watched my four grandchildren, ages 5 to 12, all wide-eyed with anticipation. I'm not certain how many times they had participated in toasts previous to this occasion, but their big eyes took in everything. They simply did what they saw others doing. With big smiles they clinked their glasses of Martinelli's sparkling cider and said, *"Skoal,"* as others were doing. Use toasts often, and you'll become accomplished at it and your family comfortable with it.

---

* *Emily Post's Etiquette.*

The warm and informal atmosphere of the buffet table puts guests at ease.

14

BUFFET ENTERTAINING

he buffet is the most popular method of entertaining today. Guests enjoy having the freedom to serve themselves as they would at home as well as the opportunity to move about. The warm and more informal atmosphere of the buffet table puts guests at ease. It is advantageous for the hosts as well because it means less work and less cleanup afterward. It also leaves the hosts freer to mingle with guests. The only thing they have to worry about is replenishing serving dishes.

Buffets fall into three categories: the true buffet, the seated buffet, and the semi-buffet. Choose the type of buffet that best suits space needs as well as the number of guests you are entertaining. But whatever type you opt for, the guests always serve themselves first and the host and hostess serve themselves last.*

The true buffet. At a true buffet the guests select their plates, food, silver, and beverages from the buffet table (see drawing). They then move to another room to sit wherever they feel comfortable. No table is set. Because guests are eating on their laps or perhaps from trays on their laps, it is best to serve foods that do not require cutting with a knife. That type of manipulation of plate, tray, and silver would be sure to end in disaster for your furniture and embarrassment for your guests. Small tables or TV trays strategically placed around the room provide guests with space for beverages. Guests may return to the buffet for seconds and dessert, or the host can remove the plates to the kitchen or designated area and serve dessert (see figure 3 in Appendix A).

The one thing worse than a quitter is a person who is afraid to begin.

The seated buffet. At a seated buffet you put only the food on the buffet table (see figure 4 in Appendix A). Guests serve themselves at the buffet table and then sit at a table set with silver, glasses, and napkins. Because your guests do not have to balance plates on their knees, you do not have to restrict the types of food offered. Your guests may return to the buffet table for dessert, or you may serve it at the table.

The semi-buffet. At a semi-buffet the host or hostess fills each plate from the buffet table and then hands it to the seated guest. Buffet entertaining is always more informal, but serving guests in this manner lends a caring and personal touch.

Special-occasion buffets. Buffets are the best way to accommodate large numbers of guests. The special-occasion buffet can be casual (as with one served outdoors on the patio, poolside, lawn, or game room area) or more elegant (as with a wedding reception served in the dining area). Buffets are a popular way to serve for the holidays, open houses, and receptions of all kinds.

Buffet Table Logistics

When planning a buffet, you must first decide which type you will use—the true, seated, or semi buffet. Next plan how traffic will flow around the buffet table. It is the key to success. The serving line must begin and end at logical points to avoid confusion and congestion.

The circular buffet. This buffet table is accessible from all four sides (see figure 5 in Appendix A). The logical starting point begins with the plates and ends with beverages.

The three-sided buffet. When space is limited, you may push the table to the wall. The plates signal the beginning point (see drawing). Check for the best traffic flow so that from the end of the buffet line guests can go directly to their seating area without having to cross through the service area again. If necessary because of limited space, place beverages on a small table beside the larger table (see figure 6 in Appendix A).

The double-line buffet. For a larger crowd, two serving lines moving on either side of a table or tables make for faster service. Both lines should have the same service plan—plates at the starting point with beverages, silver, and napkins at the end (see figure 7 in Appendix A).

Buffets can be set up wherever it is most convenient: on a breakfast bar area, a sideboard, two card tables placed together, or even on a kitchen counter for an informal potluck meal. A cloth or a table runner usually covers the table buffet. But you may also leave surfaces bare except for trivets and mats for hot dishes.

And there's nothing wrong with inviting guests to join you in the kitchen to help themselves directly from the pots and pans. While this type of serving may have little elegance about it, it certainly has its own folksy charm that will disarm even the most staid and uptight guest. Plunging into a pot and serving yourself is an intimate experience we generally share only with family. The food line will move rapidly as guests select the amount and kinds of food that please them. Generally the hosts will stay nearby to give directions and identify a casserole. Then everyone can proceed to the table already set with silver and beverages.

Disposable plates and paperware are acceptable, depending on the occasion, and preferable when serving large groups. But please, no limp plain white paper plates. Sturdy attractive paper goods are available and are designed to accent every occasion and type of decor. So regardless of the occasion, go the extra mile and invest in tasteful and inviting paperware if you decide to use it.

One problem with buffets is the tendency for men to hang back politely while allowing and encouraging women to go through first. Short of acting like a police officer, encourage partners to go through together. You'll spoil the "mix" of people unless you do. Otherwise you will have a cluster of women sitting together. Each new woman coming through line will join the existing group of women, not knowing where else to sit. The men will likewise cluster together.

Whether you have one or two lines, you need to place food in logical order so guests can serve themselves without backtracking—plates first, main course, hot foods and vegetables next, then bread, salad, and trays (if used). If you already have the bread buttered for guests, the line can move faster, or you may place the butter on the table.

When you do not seat guests at a table, you should place the flatware and napkins at the end of the table. Yet how many times I have been required to pick up napkin and flatware at the beginning of the line and carry it with me around the buffet table. The flatware either gets dropped into food or retrieved from the floor (in which case you must replace it). Spare your guests this embarrassment!

After determining where you want your buffet table, plan your centerpiece. The size of a buffet centerpiece should be in proportion to the table. Buffet tables need stronger decorations in both color and character, since guests do not linger there. First impressions must count. A centerpiece in a strong color and a cluster of matching candles would be striking. The cloth on the serving table could be a strong color also. As you plan the colors for the table, take into account the color of the room and coordinate it with the serving area. Whatever the centerpiece, it should not overwhelm the food, which is the major attraction at the buffet table.

Tips on Serving Buffet-style
- Avoid crowding things on a buffet table. Ideally you should have enough room between serving dishes so guests can put their plates down while helping themselves.

- If the buffet table is small, you may stack plates, napkins, and flatware on a nearby sideboard or table.
- A buffet table is more appealing when it looks bountiful. A basket with dinner rolls piled high is more tempting than a single layer of rolls served from a platter.
- Remove empty dishes or soon-to-be-empty dishes from the buffet table in order to maintain its appeal. You can refill the empty dish in the kitchen or replace it with a ready-and-waiting backup dish. Refilling of dishes should take place in the kitchen area, not at the buffet table.
- Think through the placement of food. Gravy should follow mashed potatoes. Butter should go next to bread or rolls. Remember that guests will have a plate in their hands and that it will be difficult to butter or cut anything.
- If necessary, enlist competent help to assist you in keeping food replenished on the buffet table.

Ideas to Enhance Buffet Serving

- For a large or just a "different" type of buffet, serve food from several areas. There could be, for example, four separate buffet stations—one in each corner of the room. One could be for the main course, one for salads and vegetables, one for beverages, and the last one for desserts.
- A "flat" buffet, one with all flat serving dishes, is visually boring. Footed platters and bowls, bread sticks standing tall in a basket, and tall candles and flowers can help achieve varied and interesting heights. An attractive do-it-yourself platter perch can be made by turning over a broad-bottomed dish and covering it with a coordinating napkin or towel. To minimize people bumping into tall items, place them toward the middle or back, out of the way of reaching hands.
- Unusual serving pieces will give your buffet originality. Rather than always serving from a conventional dish, think of

something different. How about serving butter from a seashell? Biscuits from a clay flowerpot? Fruit salad in a hollowed-out melon shell?

- Stuff silver in a crock with a cloth napkin lining.
- Silver can also be rolled in cloth napkins of two coordinating colors and placed in a large crock for easy retrieval.
- Fold napkins and lay them out in an alternating color pattern (red and white or blue and yellow, etc.). Put an assortment of napkins in a range of colors on the buffet table. Guests can then select a color that suits their mood or liking.

---

*Ideas are adapted from Betty Crocker, *Betty Crocker's Buffets,* 1st ed. (New York: Random House, 1984), and other sources.

Picnics are one of my favorite methods of entertaining.

15

PICTURE-PERFECT PICNICS

icnics, or what we might call outdoor feasts, have been popular a long time. History records that Cleopatra tempted Antony with a sumptuous banquet aboard her golden barge. However, Adam and Eve must have enjoyed a few romantic moments picnicking outdoors in their Garden of Eden.

The word "picnic" derives from the French *piquenique,* which means fashionable social entertaining in which guests contribute a share of the meal. It's the forerunner of "potluck." Today's picnic simply means a pleasurable outdoor excursion on which people take food with them to eat in the open air.

Let's extend that definition to include any meal taken away from the dining table. A picnic, then, could be any meal eaten before the coziness of a fireplace, around a Christmas tree, on a porch during a spring rain, or at a poolside table. Whether at home, the park, the beach, on a boat, or in the mountains, picnics are a great way of bringing people together for food and fun. And the out-of-doors usually provides built-in entertainment.

The word "picnic" may conjure up warm, lazy summer afternoons by a stream or under the shade of a large tree. But we should expand the concept of picnicking. Picnics can be a year-round adventure regardless of where you live or the season.

While living in Calgary we were only one and a half hours from Banff. One day when the temperature plunged to an icy 30 degrees below zero we invited fellow California friends to join us on a venture to Lake Minnewanka at Banff National Park. After we had expended considerable effort to convince them that we were serious, we all shared a great impromptu picnic in a park shelter. It wasn't half bad around a blazing fire. After the meal we explored the frozen lake and discovered scuba divers exploring the waters below the ice with battery-operated flashlights strapped to their heads! We enjoyed a great winter picnic adventure in spite of winter conditions.

Don't fret over what you'd do with your time if you could live life over again—get busy with what you have left.

Weekend afternoons provide great picnic occasions. Harry and I have a favorite spot on the King's River below Pine Flat Dam that we haunt. Over the years we have invited many friends to join us at our "air-conditioned" outdoor picnic spot. As water spills over the dam, the spray cools the air for a half mile or so. (This was a refreshing relief from Fresno's blistering summer heat—until they diverted the water to produce electricity.)

Picnics are one of my favorite methods of entertaining. I have several special picnic cloths and dishes that I can easily gather for quick and easy entertaining. Even at the last minute I can invite a few close friends along with someone outside my circle of personal friends.

Summer, winter, spring, or fall picnics are always in good taste. They can range from more formal affairs to informal family gatherings. Whatever level of formality you choose, it is a quick and easy way to entertain and a relaxed way to get to know people.

Picnic Know-how

Obviously, picnicking will run more smoothly if you take time in advance to plan for the type of picnic you will host.

Plates. Most of the time picnics call for more practical plates that are both nonbreakable and inexpensive. Some good choices are plastic, Corning ware, or enamelware. They are nicer to eat on as well as moneysaving in the long run when compared to paper products.

If you use paper plates because of their disposability, purchase the sturdy, glazed type divided into sections. Flimsy white plates that bend and dump soggy foods are definite no-no's! If you insist on using them, however, at least purchase plate holders to provide support. An attractive outdoor picnic can be served on disposable plates when colored plates are coordinated with a pretty tablecloth. But nothing can be more boring than white paper plates!

You can add a stylish touch to a picnic meal by using china. A friend invited me for a picnic to celebrate my birthday. What a delightful surprise when she spread a fancy cloth, china, candles, and flowers on the table! Picnics can be elegant too.

Glasses and cups. Plastic glasses come in a wide variety of styles, sizes, and colors. For special occasions you might want to pack crystal stemware. I find that unnecessary as I purchased look-alike plastic goblets trimmed in gold for more elegant picnic occasions, but I have pink plastic with straight octagonal sides for our trailer when we camp in the mountains.

Cups can be of the same material as the plates, the same color and pattern, or a contrasting color. You can serve hot soups and stews in insulated mugs, sturdy glazed paper bowls, or bowls to match the plates. Styrofoam cups bring mixed reviews. They are environmentally unsound, rarely attractive, blow over in an instant, yet they do keep contents hot. You decide.

Flatware. Unless your menu consists of only sandwiches and finger foods that don't require flatware, habitual picnickers need a set of silver just for picnicking. When I invested in new stainless steel flatware, I kept my old set for picnics. I also purchased a set of flatware with colored handles for special picnic occasions.

Napkins. Grocery store paper napkins make the easiest picnic choice. But think color if you choose this route. Many vibrant-colored paper products now match or coordinate with your table settings. However, cloth napkins will add a touch of class to any picnic setting. One pretty but practical napkin fabric is terry cloth. You can purchase this easy-care fabric in most fabric stores and hem it to make any size tablecloth or napkin. Or buy a supply of inexpensive washcloths the next time they're on sale. Pop them into the washer and dryer and then store them for the next picnic.

Extras. Include in your planning an interesting centerpiece—a vase for wildflowers, or a bowl for a fruit centerpiece. Even on a picnic, candles are a must for me. When burning candles outdoors, it is better to protect them with a hurricane shade. My favorite outdoor candle is one placed inside a heavy, clear glass holder. They are available in both round and square shapes. And don't forget the matches!

The picnic basket. Specially designed picnic baskets range in style and price from a more ordinary red-and-white-checked fabric that includes white plastic place settings to more extraordinarily elegant baskets containing goblets, china, and damask cloths. You can easily convert any large open basket with a handle to a pretty picnic basket with two cloth squares—one lines the basket and the other tops the picnic contents. The two cloths can then become your table covering.

Packing, Transporting, and Storing Tips

As far as possible, pack all items in reverse order of use. For example, food on the bottom, then plates and flatware, with tablecloth on top.

Containers. Hard plastic stacking containers with tight-sealing lids provide an easy way to transport your food. This way, even if a container tips, it won't spill contents. A supply of plastic bags, plastic wrap, wax paper, and foil might also come in handy.

Portable refrigeration is necessary for foods containing mayonnaise, eggs, cream, sour cream, or yogurt if it will be more than two hours until you serve the meal. You can keep ice chests and coolers cold with refreezable ice, blocks frozen in clean milk cartons, or bags of ice cubes. Heavily insulated metal coolers will keep foods cold for 24 to 48 hours. Styrofoam coolers work well for shorter periods of time. Whenever possible, carry mayonnaise in smaller containers and add it to the salad or sandwiches just prior to serving.

Styrofoam, insulated chests, and ice buckets also protect hot foods. You can keep casseroles hot by wrapping them in heavy-duty aluminum foil plus several thicknesses of newspaper that you then tape closed. Food will remain hot for 2 to 4 hours when wrapped this way. Quilted casserole carriers, baskets, and low-sided boxes make good carriers for hot foods.

Try to avoid leftovers by careful planning. But if you must bring perishable food home, place it in the ice chest immediately. Throw away any food that is questionable. It isn't worth the risk of food poisoning. Take along a plastic garbage bag for disposal of all garbage when the event is over.

Picnic Presentation Ideas

Food seems to taste better when eaten outdoors close to nature. But you can enjoy it even more when you give special attention to its presentation. Even though picnics will always be more informal than a dining room, table settings and food presentation can and should be just as attractive. Here are some ideas to get your creative juices flowing. Hopefully, you'll hardly be able to wait for your next picnic![1]

- Set your picnic on an Oriental rug, a quilt from the past, a raffia mat, or a designer sheet rather than on an old blanket.
- Accent your picnic with fresh flowers or a flowering plant set in a basket.
- Glamorize your picnic table with hurricane lamps. The shades protect the flame from the breeze.

- Roll flatware inside a large dinner napkin that coordinates with your color scheme (especially if you are using plastic so it won't blow away). Such flatware bundles are easy to un-pack and set at each place.
- Marinated veggies and other goods can show off their beauty in old-fashioned glass canning jars.

Manners are the happy way of doing things.
EMERSON

- Create a delectable edible centerpiece with fresh fruit (apples, nectarines, peaches, plums, strawberries, bananas, and grapes) arranged in a wicker basket.
- If you have a campfire, serve fruit kabobs for dessert; alternate marshmal-lows, cubes of pound cake, and pineapple chunks on a skewer and grill until lightly browned.
- The sandwich is a favorite picnic meal. For a fun version of the oversized "Hero Sandwich" (also called sub or hoagie, de-pending on what part of the country you live in), slice a very long loaf of bread horizontally and place on a board cut to shape. Spread halves with any selected fillings. A clever serv-ing idea is to place wide planks end to end and cover with heavy-duty aluminum foil. Placed in the center of this long narrow table, the sandwich serves as a centerpiece. All you need to add are napkins. The foil serves a triple purpose—as a plate, a table covering, and an aid in easy cleanup. When the picnic is over, roll up the foil and toss. Many bakeries will prepare six-foot loaves of bread. You can serve large crowds in this manner.
- For a Western meal and theme, use blue denim jean material for a tablecloth. Colorful bandannas make great place mats or napkins. Since I am a quilter, I have made a blue denim jean memory quilt of fabric saved from the jeans of my daughter's four boys. From the same bandanna fabric that I used to back the quilt I have made napkins. If you want to go all out for this

look, serve on enamelware dishes using small galvanized buckets as salad bowls and tiny ones as candleholders. This is showstopping stuff!

- A violet sprigged tablecloth with linen napkins of royal purple is striking against the green of a lawn and yard. Rather than a centerpiece in the center of the table, you might hang your centerpiece from a limb over the table so that it just clears the top of the table. Another idea is to use a decorative birdcage filled with purple violets and small-leafed ivy cascading over the edges.

- A picnic either by day or by night can be an exciting adventure for two. Pack your basket and spread a tempting array of food in your favorite secluded spot. I just returned from the Cayman Islands, where a couple had a table for two set up on the sand at dusk. The setting, good food, stunning sunset, and candlelight made for an alluring, romantic picnic.

- For a picnic on the beach, experiment with a nautical theme, especially if you have just returned from an exotic vacation. I purchased a square of material with white sailboats and anchors on a red background. A hurricane candle set in sand with starfish and shells scattered about carries out the theme. White or blue plates with red, white, or blue napkins would be perfect.

- Adorn a picnic table with a watering can filled with sprays of forsythia.

- A cluster of fragrant flowers from the garden or the local market can make any outdoor meal fun. Accent the table with votive candles inside miniature galvanized pails along with colored-handled garden tools and a pair of colorful garden gloves. Use the garden tools as salad servers. Let your imagination go. Pure fun!

- My daughter Carlene used a "love basket" idea to get some time with her doctor-husband during his residency. In order to increase their time together, she'd pack up the kids and a supper and meet him at the hospital. He was able to slip out for a few minutes on occasion, and they'd eat together on the hospital grounds. It took a great deal of effort on her part. Fellow residents took notice and dubbed her "the wife with the love basket." Brian, phlegmatic husband that he is, rarely commented. But Carlene decided that if she had to be known as something, then "the wife with the love basket" wasn't a bad title.[2] (See Appendix B.)

During the summer Harry and I park our trailer on property near the southern entrance to Yosemite National Park. The cool mountain air, large sequoias, and dense foilage provide a retreat when we need to get away from it all.

A sizable portion of my entertaining, especially during the summer months, takes place here, out-of-doors, at our summer camp site. Sometimes we invite guests to share the beauty of this spot with us. On such occasions I plan carefully and have everything on hand. Even though it is a campsite, I try to entertain with style. I use a pink plastic cloth with a voile appearance, black plastic place mats with pink roses on them, and pink plastic plates. The centerpiece is one a florist friend of mine surprised me with after I entertained her and another friend. Taking pine cones, pieces of bark, wood, and lichen from the spot where we had camped, she blended them all into a unique table arrangement by adding pink roses and a votive candle glued in the center.

Sometimes I invite others who are camping for the weekend to join us for a special after-church meal, a Saturday night wiener roast around the campfire, or even a hearty Sunday morning brunch—all impromptu. Since the nearest town is 15 miles away, this calls for a little advance planning on my part, so I always have an emergency meal or two on hand—and have had to use them several times. But we meet new people and develop friendships that we wouldn't ever have otherwise.

This summer I planned a surprise birthday party for the brunch bunch there. I invited a large group (14 adults and 4 children) and wanted it simple yet attractive and memorable. My daughter Carlene was visiting, and together we came up with a theme—sunflowers—perfect for an outdoor setting and coordinated everything around it.

We used three picnic tables, two for guests and one for food. A light blue disposable cloth purchased from a party supplier covered each table. Brilliant blue plastic plates rested on bright yellow paper place mats. (Such place mats cost only a few pennies each. Each plate had a sunflower paper napkin. A basket of fresh and silk sunflowers completed the theme.

If you sow kindness, you will reap a crop of friends.

The food—furnished potluck—was all typical brunch items with the addition of a purchased cake decorated with sunflowers. The food tasted even better because we were all hungry and because we ate it out-of-doors with the splender of Yosemite as a perfect backdrop.

You may not have a moutain hideaway like ours, but you can use the opportunities you do have for outdoor entertaining—a backyard picnic, a trip to the beach, to a park, or to the mountains—summer, winter, spring, or fall. It is simply a great way to become the hospitable encourager to someone who needs you, and you don't even have to clean house first!

---

[1] Ideas are from *The Complete Book of Picnics* (Ortho Books, 1979).
[2] The Love Basket idea is adapted from a seminar presented by Emily Barnes.

Fellowship dinners can bring the church family together.

16

CREATIVE CHURCH POTLUCKS

ellowship dinners can bring the church family to-gether and enable them to show hospitality to new members and guests. A feast offered to those visiting the church can be a means of friendship evangelism. Such meals not only provide a social get-together, but can also serve as an opportune means of nutrition education. Many people trace their first exposure to vegetarian cooking at a church fellowship dinner. With a little planning we can reduce the liabilities these dinners pose and yet retain and multiply fellowship opportunities.

Potluck Etiquette

Will Cuppy says, "Etiquette is behaving yourself a little bit better than is absolutely necessary." And that's exactly how church members should be conducting themselves at fellowship dinners. In order to accomplish this goal, it becomes necessary for leaders to retrain members so that they can fully use the potential of fellowship dinners.

Ideally, a planning committee should organize these dinners so they will be the exemplary meals they can be. A committee consisting of both new and longtime church members and a tactful chairperson can tailor a plan that will meet the needs of a particular congregation. When formulating new plans, however, and attempting to change some habits that may have become deeply ingrained, remember to make haste slowly. Don't, for example, just suddenly announce no more desserts. A less radical approach is necessary if the church has been having an over-large dessert table for fellowship meals. The potluck planning committee will function better if broken down into cochairpersons in charge of various aspects of planning. I suggest two chairpersons—one overseeing decorations and the other in charge of food service and cleanup. The committee should be large enough so that members can share jobs. No one person should be stuck with cleanup every time. Dividing jobs into manageable portions according to talents and abilities keeps people from dreading their turn.

No matter what scales we use, we never know the weight of another person's burden.

Through church newsletters and bulletin announcements ask church members to deliver food to the church kitchen table-ready. Hot dishes should be prebaked and wrapped with newspaper to be kept warm; salads made and wrapped with saran wrap and ready to serve; bread buttered; cakes cut, etc. This makes for promptness in serving as well as less work for servers.

In order to assure sufficient food for guests as well as church members, ask couples to furnish two dishes that will each feed 10 to 12; singles, one dish to serve 10 to 12. A family should furnish an extra dish for every two children they bring.

Deacons should set up tables and chairs immediately following church service if they have not been put in place during the week. Having them put in place beforehand also allows the decorating person time to complete the tables in advance. Most of the churches I have visited have either six- or eight-foot rectangular tables. But round tables promote conversation and fellowship more easily than rectangular tables, where the persons at the other end cannot be seen nor heard. My home church in Fresno has round tables. They are no more difficult to store and have been an excellent investment from the start. Round tables are excellent for dinners of all kinds, wedding receptions, and banquets.

Tablecloths enhance the decor of the room and the beauty of the meal. You can purchase wipe-off plastic cloths with a taffeta appearance. They come in many colors and last for years. You can add additional cloths in other colors and for other occasions over the years. My home church has white linen cloths for banquet occasions that members can rent. They must check them out and return them clean and pressed.

Simple table decorations such as paper place mats, a single flower in a vase, a candle, fresh-cut ivy clipped from the yard, and fall leaves all add to the overall appearance of the table. Let's remember that when we invite guests to a fellowship meal, it is similar to inviting guests to our home. When guests visit our homes, we make certain preparations in an attempt to have things as nice as we possibly can. Fellowship meals may have to be simpler than similar home preparations because of the number of persons being served, but, nevertheless, the tables should and can have simple but special touches to make them attractive.

It is better to ask visitors to remain at the church for dinner rather than trying to get them to drive to the home of a family they do not know. Most people feel uncomfortable when invited into the home of someone they have never met before. It also keeps them from getting to know the pastor as well as other members.

With the aid of some good planning, a fellowship dinner can and should be served promptly after the close of the church service. However, no fellowship dinner crew should have to miss the church service in order to have the meal ready. If all dishes have been brought ready to serve, last-minute preparations will be at a minimum. By carefully utilizing the time between services, your church can have the meal on the table 15 to 20 minutes after the close of the service.

Appoint hosts for each fellowship dinner. They should greet guests and members as they enter the social hall or eating area, obtaining the names of guests and assisting in getting people seated comfortably. Introduce the visitors to the others at the table and leave them in the hands of caring church members who can converse as creatively with the guests as they would were the people visiting in their own home.

Friendship always benefits.

Sacred music playing softly will cover up background noise and lend reverence to the occasion. It will also serve as a reminder of the sacredness of the hours. Instrumental music is preferable to singing for reasons we have mentioned previously.

Provide an activity for small children while they wait to be served rather than allowing them to run wild. Some suggestions might include a story corner where they could listen to story cassettes or watch a Sabbath video, or they could color pictures or place mats where they sit. Parents (as well as others) will greatly appreciate this.

Just before the food is served, the host should welcome everyone, using a microphone if necessary so that all may hear clearly. Introduce guests by name with a sentence or two of interest about them in the same manner as if they were being presented to a friend. This will give others a point of reference from which they can make conversation and be friendly. If a special group is being honored, this is the time for recognition and appreciation to be given.

Instruct everybody how the serving will take place and offer prayer. The hosts may then dismiss the people by tables, allowing those with guests to go first. Avoid asking guests only to go first, as this means they return to eat alone while the rest of their table waits in line.

An adult should always accompany children when they go through the food lines. Ask or instruct people to limit themselves to one dessert so that all may enjoy a selection.

The church must supply plates, cups, and flatware for guests. It is helpful when the church itself provides paper goods for everyone attending. This makes for less mess and for easier cleanup afterward.

Two long tables placed end to end allow easier and faster service. People can form two lines and serve themselves from both sides. Large churches could use four tables to speed things up.

While someone makes announcements and introductions, others place the food on the tables by categories—entrées first, followed by vegetables and salads—in that order. You can hold some dishes back to ensure enough food for the last to be served. Also rotate dishes as needed.

Set the tables up in the following manner: Put plates before the entrées. Place silver and napkins at the far end of the table for people to pick up last. This avoids having to juggle these items when serving yourself. Another attractive way to handle this matter is to have the silver and napkins already at each place just as you would at home at a seated buffet. Organize desserts on a separate table and have them dispensed by a server, one selection per person.

Place a pitcher of water at each table along with glasses for easy service. Slices of lemon in the water add a special touch.

Ask people to clear their own tables and assist with cleanup following the meal. When you use paper and plastic goods, designate someone to clear the table and place all trash in receptacles provided. Have someone wipe the table clean. All this could be handled under the direction of a host appointed at each table.

Most churches have monthly fellowship dinners. Encourage mini-fellowship dinners on other Sabbaths. Two or three families or singles can form a team and host dinners at the church for guests. Even if no guests come, they can still enjoy fellowship together.

Creative Ideas for Fellowship Dinners

- When weather allows, move fellowship dinners to a local park for a delightful change.
- Plan dinner around a theme: Christmas, Thanksgiving, spring, an ethnic meal, or a soup and salad bar. Background music, table decorations, and food should fit the theme.
- Feature a specific type of entrée at the dinner. For example, have vegetarian patties with gravy, encouraging members to use their own recipe. They can exchange recipes with each other.
- Feature a planned potluck in which the committee selects in advance the recipes it would like the people to bring and prints them in the church newsletter or bulletin.
- Feature an annual Thanksgiving or Christmas dinner. Preplan the menu. A host is responsible for decorating the table and providing eight place settings. The host seats the guests at tables and serves them.
- Have a mixer activity while people are waiting to be served or use it following the dinner.
- Rather than just asking one person to pray, ask three persons to pray for three different things. For example, one might pray for fellowship among the people present, a second for a special blessing from God on the people of God, and a third give thanks for the food.
- Instead of just saying the prayer, ask everyone to sing a prayer.
- Appoint a host at each table to direct conversation.
- Plan theme fellowship dinners, spotlighting various groups within the church, such as new members by baptism (provide name tags and sing "I'm So Glad I'm a Part of the Family of God"), new members by transfer, the elderly, singles, teenagers, or college students home for holidays. Have a church officers appreciation day for church staff and division leaders (provide name tags with office currently held, how

long in office). Have everyone write a note of appreciation to the leaders.

- After the fellowship dinner, have a sing-along, testimonies, mission story with slides or videos taken by a member on a recent trip to a mission field, etc.

Quick Table Decorating Magic

- Fresh-cut green ivy cut from a yard makes a beautiful centerpiece. Place strands down the center of the table to form a continuous chain. For a special touch, place pink carnations among the ivy. Use pink paper place mats to carry out the color scheme.
- Float three camellias in a low, clear bowl during their blooming season. Use color-coordinated place mats.
- Purchase yellow and blue primroses in four-inch pots during the early spring. Wrap colorful coordinating paper around the pot and tie with a bow. Use alternating yellow and blue place mats and napkins around the table.
- During the fall season use treated fall leaves in the center of the table. Scatter among the leaves nuts in their shells, gourds, Indian corn, and mini pumpkins. Use alternating brown and orange paper place mats and napkins around the table.
- Lanterns add a decorative touch for the holidays. A gold lantern with a tea light or votive candle for each table presents a festive appearance. Fresh holiday greenery completes the scene.
- Lay shredded foil down the center of the table. Then take yards of curling ribbon, curl it and snip into three-inch pieces, and scatter them over the shredded foil. Sprinkle with foil confetti.
- For the new year, purchase party hats. Put one or two per table and sprinkle confetti on the table. Bowls of party mix are a nice added touch.
- Spread bags of colored shredded paper down the center of the table and sprinkle jelly beans throughout. Especially good for

spring decor.

- To honor graduates, feature their class colors in the place mats. Stretch crepe paper ribbon, also in class colors, down the center of the table. Add a paper graduation cap as a centerpiece. The extra mile would be to make paper diplomas by rolling paper and tying them with gold string.

You can purchase paper place mats by the hundreds. Buy them in many colors and store them in an organized manner in a supply cupboard. Save lanterns, candles, candleholders, vases, and other supplies that you accumulate over the years. Remember, a fellowship dinner replaces inviting people into your home. It should be approached with the same caring spirit and personal flair as you would at home—only on a larger scale.

A blue enamelware coffeepot holds red silk tulips as the centerpiece.

THE PRIME-TIME FAMILY HOUR

he last frontier for families, in most homes, is the dinner hour. In the past it was the time families connected and children learned most family values. But too many children are coming home today to an empty house with a note on the fridge that reads "I'll be home late tonight. There's a TV dinner in the freezer. Love, Mom."

The family dinner hour is much more than receiving a quota of vitamins, minerals, proteins, and carbohydrates to fuel our bodies. It is a time for touching lives, telling the news of the day, bragging about successes, sharing hurts, and receiving comfort from those who love you. Dinner is a time for laying plans for tomorrow and sharing good times together.

The days of *Father Knows Best,* which sported a stay-at-home mom who took care of the house and had a meal ready at 5:00 every day, are mostly gone. But a family's need to connect and share is not.

It's time to revitalize the dinner hour and make it prime-time hour at your house. Let's look at how to do it.*

Involve everyone in dinner preparation. A survey of working mothers found that 77 percent prepared dinner alone and 64 percent handled cleanup alone. Yet these same mothers probably complain that they don't have enough time to spend with their children.

Each family needs to dream up some creative ways of involving the children in preparation and cleanup. Rather than leaving the kitchen and having them do it alone, or worse yet having your family leave the kitchen and you doing it alone, work side by side with them. While you are working together you can be spending some quality time in some heart-to-heart sharing.

Create a friendly atmosphere. No one can eat and enjoy a meal if someone is barking out commands like "You eat just like a pig. . . . Don't talk with your mouth full. . . . Sit up straight. . . ."

People perceive all such comments as criticism. Criticism and eating don't go together. It causes indigestion and will make the children prefer to eat in front of the TV or in their rooms alone.

Above all, don't use the dinner hour as lecture hour. It is no time to speak to the children about grades, behavior, cleaning their rooms, or doing homework. Such things may need to be discussed, but not at mealtime.

Turn off the television. A New York *Times* and CBS News poll showed that in families with children under 18 years of age, 42 percent spend the dinner hour watching TV! Even worse, it found that children who microwave their own dinners sit in front of the TV while eating and thus completely lose the importance of eating with others. Television is a major distraction during mealtime. It is impossible to have meaningful conversation around the table when eyes and ears are glued to the magic box. The "No TV during meals" rule may be just as hard for Dad or Mom to follow if they use it to unwind after a difficult day or to catch the news. But it must be done. You are losing precious hours of time with your children to television.

Television became a real problem in our home when our last teenager was still living with us. We didn't watch it during meals, but as soon as he had scarfed down his last bite, he'd excuse himself in preference for TV. Harry and I discussed how to handle it, and decided on a revolutionary experiment. When Mark came home the next day, the TV had vanished. He stormed, fumed, and staged a general scene, but an amazing thing happened after supper. He lingered at the table to play the Ungame with us again and again.

Sometimes we forgot the Ungame and just talked. Other times he'd play racquetball with a friend. Interaction with live people began once we got the TV under control. It was one of the best things we could have done for Mark, but one of the hardest on ourselves. We had to break our own habit of watching a show or two before retiring.

Limit interruptions. Humorist Erma Bombeck sums it up succinctly. This mother of three says, "We had two rules at our house. The first was: 'Either show up for dinner or bring a note from God excusing you.' The second: 'Absolutely no one uses the phone while we're eating.'"

Offer hospitality to one another without grumbling.
1 PETER 4:9

This sounds easy, but how do you accomplish it when you have five people headed in different directions? When kids hit a certain age and begin with youth meetings, parties, friends, intramurals, choir practice, committee meetings, and the like, weeks can go by before you have a semblance of a meal together.

If mealtime is to be priority, we have to be there. When it can't be a reality every night in your home, try for five or four out of the week if that is reasonable for your lifestyle. Then cut out all activities that interfere on those evenings. No exceptions!

The phone can also cause havoc during meals. If you have an answering machine, let it ring. If you can't handle not answering a ringing phone, have someone answer and say, "We're having dinner right now. We'll call you back just as soon as we're finished."

Develop the art of communication. We've agreed not to criticize the children for poor table manners. Now what do we talk about? A "What happened today at school, son?" may draw little more than "Nothing." But children who hear their parents explore interesting subjects, share stories, and discuss politics, current events, and the news of the day will be more likely to do so too.

Elinor Ochs, a UCLA applied-linguistics professor who has studied dinner customs and conversations, says the most successful dinner hours involve storytelling. So rather than asking a child to tell you something interesting, relate to him or her something interesting that happened during your own day. Teach by example. Begin by describing to your child all the little funny or interesting things that go on in your world. Save a good joke to share, an interesting current event, or a news item from TV.

In some families all this talk will lead to animated discussions that everyone will thoroughly enjoy. But make sure everyone gets included rather than one person dominating.

Develop family traditions. Mealtime is one of the best times to develop meaningful family traditions. It could be the children taking turns offering a blessing on the food, or Father praying first followed by one child. Perhaps it could be holding hands during prayer, or even reciting or singing a prayer together. Such a practice reminds everyone to be thankful for God's blessings and sets a tone of relaxed togetherness.

The closing of the meal can be just as important. Do family members rush off in different directions the minute they have chowed down their portion of food? You may need to instigate a new rule that everyone stays at the table until the meal is over.

This is a great time to have a short family worship. Rather than letting everyone scatter to play, to friends' houses, to TV, or to homework, and then attempting to gather them again, try family worship now. You are all together, facing one another around the table—excellent positioning for interaction. Read a Bible verse or a story that illustrates the verse, and then go for a discussion of how that applies to our lives today. Kneel together for a short family prayer. Add a family hug in which you stand in a circle with your arms around one another.

Encourage good table manners. Encourage good manners not by sharp criticism but by modeling them yourself. Your children will eventually eat the way you do. Now, that's a scary thought! Play the Dinner Game. It teaches players to pay attention to the needs of others and to help meet those needs. You can play the game anytime the entire family is together for dinner. Here are the rules:

1. You cannot ask for anything for yourself.

2. Watch for the needs of the person seated to your left. Try to notice what he or she might lack and ask the person you are watching what he or she wants.

3. You get what you want or need from the person on your right.

4. Remember to say "Please" and "Thank you."

The leader of the Dinner Game is the servant of all the players. To make the game flow more smoothly, the leader should sit to the left of the person who might need the most help. When dinner ends, the leader also helps with cleanup. After your family has become good at playing the Dinner Game, you might want to include your friends.

In addition, you could instigate a Good Manners Meal once a week or month. This could be a meal served in the dining room on china with candles, etc. Males would take turns seating females. Here is where you would teach how to put napkins in the lap, which fork to use, how to pass food, and other manners. The role of host could rotate so the children learn to observe the needs of guests and to initiate and steer conversation.

Practice table setting skills. Your home is the place to experiment with your new table setting skills. It is unrealistic for most women to set the table in Martha Stewart style every night of the week. A more manageable goal might be to begin with one night a week. You might have a creative and interesting table setting for Friday evening.

In one seminar I demonstrate a colorful and fun setting for a family with small children. First I lay down a red, white, and blue country checked tablecloth. Then I set the table with navy-blue enamelware plates and bowls, red plastic glasses, and red-handled silverware. A blue enamelware coffeepot holds red silk tulips as the centerpiece. Two red candlesticks hold navy candles. Red cloth napkins complete the picture.

The few ideas I present in the seminar prime the minds of those attending, and soon people are coming up with dozens of creative table settings to make Friday night supper special.

> *Much of the character of every man may be read in his house.*
> JOHN RUSKIN

Food traditions can be started by repeating family favorites every Friday night. For the Van Pelt family it has always been tostadas, grape juice, and ice cream in the summer and corn soup and muffins in the winter. Our Sabbath candle, a candle lit at no other time than Friday evening, holds center stage. The meal is simple but special, and has created lasting and treasured memories. Even now when children return for a weekend visit with their families, they expect those same traditions to continue. In some mysterious way it connects adult children to their past—which is important to their future.

You too can begin one night a week by giving the same old table a new look. Try a new cloth, folding the napkins in a different way, or using a specially created centerpiece, a new and colorful place mat, or a new or different set of dishes. Test your new ideas out on your family. Then use your most successful ones for entertaining others.

Don't give up on the idea, however, just because your family doesn't like, or worse yet, never even notices that you have done something different. I almost always use an "instant arrangement" on the kitchen table (two small pots of fresh flowers set in a basket with some greenery). Last fall I'd arranged some burnt orange mums with some green ivy that I thought was particularly striking.

Over the flickering glow of two votive candles and the new arrangement, I asked Harry if he liked it. "Oh, are they real?" he asked, reaching to touch them. He hadn't even noticed.

Even though some in our family may not recognize the effort we've made to make our everyday tables attractive, still continue to do it daily. I do it for myself, not just for my family. And I do it because it makes me feel different about my home, the table, the meal I'm serving, and because I am striving for excellence in all things.

It may be a small matter, but those fresh flowers on the table make a statement about me and how I feel about my home. I am striving for excellence—not to exhaust myself in any way, but to bring honor to my Creator so that I might more fully be able to fulfill the command to "practice hospitality" even with my family.

Daily practice in setting a table correctly and attractively will provide increased confidence for when you entertain guests. You might think of everyday meals as a dress rehearsal for entertaining. Use your best everyday creations as a springboard to developing even more fun and innovative table settings for guests. Remember, it's the personal touches you add that give your table setting flair and add a touch of pizzazz!

---

* Ideas are from Harriet Webster, "The Most Important Hour in a Child's Day" *Reader's Digest,* August 1993.

ENTERTAINMENT

Guests	Time/Date	Dinner/Party Type	Menu	Decorations/Centerpiece/Tablecloth

Games/Entertainment	Dress	Help: Hired/Voluntary		Misc. Notes

ENTERTAINMENT

Guests	Time/Date	Dinner/Party Type	Menu	Decorations/Centerpiece/Tablecloth
Van Vrankens	4:00 p.m.	Xmas Dinner Party	dressing casserole	white basket with red balls
Moores			Island meatballs	red cloth
Myers			Noodles Romanoff	greenery & mini lights
Bramhams			molded salad	red candles
Waynes			drink (holiday)	yards of red plaid ribbon
Robertsons (Pastor)			Xmas dessert	garlands of red stars
Machochs			nuts/candies	
			cheeseball/crackers	
			green pea salad	stunning!
			snowballs	
			cranberry bread	
			dinner rolls	

Games/Entertainment	Dress	Help: Hired/Voluntary	Misc. Notes
Find Someone			
Scavenger Hunt			
Puzzle			
Gift Exchange			
Carol Singing			

Figure 1

Table set for family-style service

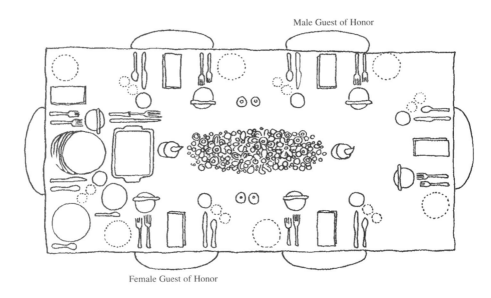

Male Guest of Honor

Female Guest of Honor

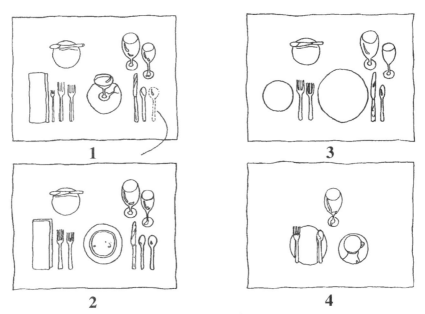

1

2

3

4

Figure 2

Figure 3

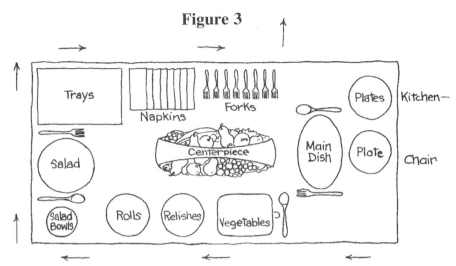

THE TRUE BUFFET. The buffet table with food, silver, plates as well as trays, napkins, and silver. Guests pick up trays from the table or move to areas around the home to eat with the trays on their laps or near tables which have been set up. No dining table is set.

Figure 4

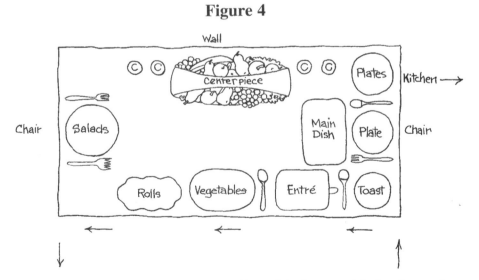

THE SEATED BUFFET. The buffet table is set with food, serving silver, and plates. Guests serve themselves and move to the dining table which has been set with silver, glasses, and napkins.

Figure 5

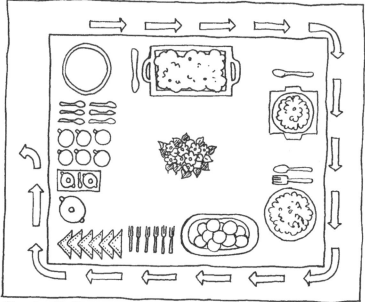

Circular Buffet

Figure 6

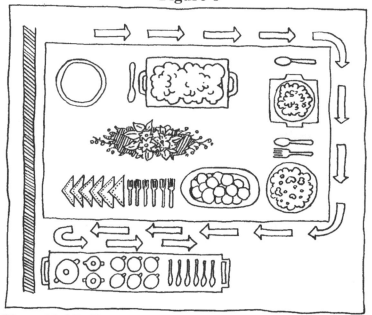

Three-sided Buffet

Figure 7

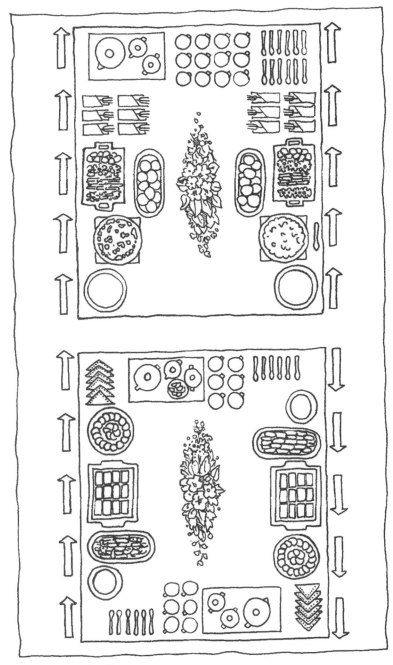

Double-line Buffet

The Love Basket—A Special Way to Say "I Care"

The Love Basket idea is a creative way of saying "I love you" to special people in your life—a husband, mother, or father, child, friend. It can be filled with food and used to say "I love you" to a husband on an anniversary; "You are special" on a birthday; or "I care" to a friend you wish to honor. The Love Basket can be elegant with china, goblets, tall candles; more simple with pretty paper goods that match the occasion; or a theme picnic—a teddy bear's picnic. It can be used for a dinner in the park or mountains or at the beach. Or it can be a surprise lunch at the office, or romantic rendezvous, the bedroom or the backyard. The objective is to create lasting memories with someone you love.

Be original, make it fun—and elegant!

Supplies needed:
1   large basket with handles
1   tablecloth (print, checked, gingham, flowered, lace, etc.)
place mats (optional)
plates/silver
napkins or coordinating fabric (napkin rings if desired)
goblets (stem, clear, or colored with stem)
2   elegant candle holders
2   tall candles (to match your color theme)
1   vase with a rose or a bunch of daisies
tape recorder and recorded music
Optional: card or gift for the occasion

Food suggestions:
French bread
variety of cheeses
grapes/fruit
sparkling cider
or Sundance Raspberry Sparkler
previously prepared main dish
potato salad
sub sandwiches
Pita bread sandwiches
raw veggies with dip
hot dogs and buns
order take out food

A SEVEN WEEK STUDY GUIDE FOR CREATIVE HOSPITALITY

Week 1: Read Chapters 2, 3, 4
    Complete lesson 1: Hospitality: Friendship Evangelism
      at Its Best

Week 2: Read Chapter 5
    Complete lesson 2: Hospitality Versus Entertaining

Week 3: Read Chapters 6 and 7
    Complete lesson 3: The Art of Making Guests Feel Welcome

Week 4: Read Chapter 8
    Complete lesson 4: Being a Good Guest

Week 5: Read Chapters 9 to 15
    Complete lesson 5: Unique Opportunities for Women

Week 6: Read Chapter 16
    Complete lesson 6: Fellowship Dinners With a Purpose

Week 7: Read Chapter 17
    Complete lesson 7: Hospitality at Home

Lesson 1

Hospitality—Friendship Evangelism at Its Best

1. The Bible clearly teaches us to practice hospitality. See Titus 1:8, 9; Romans 12: 13; 1 Peter 4:9-11.
   a. Who were these verses directed to?
   b. Does your church as a whole "practice hospitality?"
   c. Are individuals within your church practicing hospitality?
   d. What difference would it make in your church if the admonition were followed?

2. The Bible instructs us specifically to entertain "strangers" (Heb. 13:2). Who are "strangers?"
   How can this Biblical admonition be carried out today?
   What might happen as a result of entertaining "strangers?"
   Is it possible you may have entertained an angel? If so, share something about your experience.

3. Matt. 5:47 (TLB) says: If you are friendly only to your friends, how are you different from anyone else? Even the heathen do that. Did Jesus mean we should not invite our friends over? If not, what point was He making?

4. Using the previous verses as your guide, how might you extend hospitality to:
   a. a church member whose spouse is an unbeliever?
   b. a single parent who lives in your neighborhood?
   c. a family at church who is new to the area?
   d. a new family in your neighborhood?
   e. a co-worker who doesn't attend any church?

5. As a result of today's lesson I will . . .

Lesson 2

HOSPITALITY VERSUS ENTERTAINING

A book written for lawyer's wives advises that to be an asset to a husband's practice, the wife should join every organization she can and entertain as much as possible because it is important to make friends with the right people.

1. If your purpose is to "entertain," who might you invite to your home? Why?

2. Name some ways you have observed people attempting to impress their guests.

Karen Mains writes: "Entertaining says, 'I want to impress you with my beautiful home, my clever decorating, my gourmet cooking' . . . Entertaining looks for payment . . . Hospitality, however, seeks to minister. It says, 'This home is not mine. It is truly a gift from my Master. I am His servant and I use it as He desires.' Hospitality does not try to impress, but to serve."

3. Entertaining can make you more vulnerable to embarrassment than hospitality. How might this happen?

4. Share an experience, if possible, when you tried to make an impression, you flopped and were embarrassed.

5. The Shunammite woman welcomed Elisha into her home. What do you think her motive was? See 2 Kings 4:8-17.
   a. How was she blessed by showing hospitality?
   b. Give an example of how you have been blessed by extending hospitality to someone?

6. Share some ideas on how you would handle the situation if your home was unprepared for surprise guests.

7. Share some easy entertaining ideas that you have observed or used.

8. As a result of today's lesson I will . . .

Lesson 3

THE ART OF MAKING GUESTS FEEL WELCOME

1. A good host knows how to converse with guests, but more importantly, knows how to draw guests out and minister to felt needs. Discuss how a host could benefit from advice given in Prov. 10:19; 17:9; 17:13; 17:28; 20:3; 20:19; 25:11; Eccl. 10:12, 13; Phil. 2:3, 4. Make a list of negative and positive traits.

2. A good host knows how to draw guests out with sensitivity. Give a response to each statement—one that shows sensitivity and one that would likely turn a guest off. See Prov. 20:5.
   a. I find church boring.
   b. I've been very discouraged lately.
   c. More women should have abortions. There are too many people in the world as it is.

3. When Abraham parted with his guests, he made them feel cared for. Describe what he did that was special (see Gen. 18:16). What is there about eating together that binds people together?

4. The most meaningful moments in extending hospitality to others may occur when guests leave. A handshake, a hug, and walking a guest to the car often prolongs the visit and shows caring. In those parting moments confidences can be shared that would not be shared under normal circumstances. Brainstorm some ideas on how to say goodbye to guests to make them feel special, loved, and valued.

Action Assignment: How good are you at noticing the needs of those around you? The Dinner Game teaches players to pay attention to the needs of others and help meet those needs. You can play the game any time the entire family is together for dinner. These are the rules:

　　1. You cannot ask for anything for yourself (simple, but not easy).

2. Watch for the needs of the person seated to your left. Try to notice every need and ask the person you are watching what they want.
3. You get what you want or need from the person to your right.
4. Remember to say "Please" and "Thank you."

The leader of the Dinner Game is the servant of all the players. To make the game flow more smoothly, the leader should sit to the left of the person who might need the most help. When dinner ends, the leader also helps with cleanup. After your family has become good at playing the Dinner Game, you might want to include your friends.

Lesson 4

BEING A GOOD GUEST

1. What does Jesus teach about being a good guest in Luke 4:38, 39? Be creative and specific.

2. Should we accept invitations to social gatherings and dinner parties that will include mostly people who are not church members or even Christians? See Luke 5:27-32.

3. Suppose you have relatives, business associates, or acquaintances who do not like you. How can the verses in Luke 6:27-32 be applied to being a good guest in their home?

4. Should we ever drop in unannounced or invite ourselves to someone's home? See Luke 19:1-9.

5. How can you tell if you are visiting too often or staying too long? See Prov. 25:17. Brainstorm some polite ways of handling people who do this to you.

6. In John 13:2-9 why do you think Peter had difficulty accepting Christ's hospitality?
   Why is it important to learn to be served?
   Do you ever feel like Peter? Why?

7. Recall an occasion when you were a guest and felt particularly welcome in someone's home. What was it that gave you that feeling?

8. Recall an occasion when you were a guest and felt unwelcome or uncomfortable. What was it that contributed to your discomfort?

9. List at least four things that make you feel "welcome" as a guest.

Action Assignment: Being a good guest demands a written note of appreciation when hospitality has been extended to you. Let's practice today by writing a note of appreciation to someone who has welcomed you into their home recently or someone who has ministered to you in some special way. When expressing gratitude, be sure to mention at least one specific thing you particularly appreciated.

Lesson 5

HOSPITALITY: UNIQUE OPPORTUNITIES FOR WOMEN

1. Read 1 Timothy 5:4-15. This instruction was given to the early church to care for widows. What portions of the Scripture might be applicable today?

   a. What do verses 4 and 8 say about the example of hospitality before children?

   b. The importance of showing hospitality to others? (verse 10)

   c. Some women's groups have come under scorn as shown in verse 10. But such groups could dispense a great deal of support. What attributes might make the difference in a group? (see Ephesians 4:29).

2. Practicing hospitality with new believers. Read Luke 14:12-14. (NOTE: This parable was "sandwiched" between two banquet parables. Could there be any significance here?)

   a. Is it possible to mix church members with those who are not members? How might this best be done?

   b. At what type of an event would you plan to mix groups of churched and unchurched people?

   c. What type of menu might you plan?

   d. What special touches could you add to a home to create an atmosphere that says "Welcome"?

   e. If you were to invite someone outside "your group" to your home, who would it be?

3. Read Luke 10:38-42.

   a. Discuss the "Martha syndrome" that revolves around "preparation."

   b. Discuss Mary who sat at the Lord's feet.

   c. If Christ were to stop by your home for a visit, would you be more inclined to be a Martha or a Mary?

   d. What was meant by "Mary has chosen what is better"?

"The 'one thing' that Martha needed was a calm, devotional spirit, a deeper anxiety for knowledge concerning the future, immortal life, and the graces necessary for spiritual advancement. She needed less anxiety for the things which pass away, and more for those things which endure forever . . . There is a wide field for the Marthas . . . But let them first sit with Mary at the feet of Jesus" *(The Desire of Ages,* p. 509).

5. How might we be more like Mary who sat at Jesus' feet and yet get the preparation done also?

Action Assignment

a. Plan to entertain sometime within the next four weeks. Include on your guest list a new believer, a coworker, or someone outside your circle of friends.

b. A creative touch I can add to my table tonight is _____ .

Lesson 6

FELLOWSHIP DINNERS WITH A PURPOSE

1. Read Luke 14:12 and make five observations about these verses.
   a.
   b.
   c.
   d.
   e.

2. List several purposes for fellowship dinners.

3. How are visitors cared for in your church when there is no fellowship dinner?

4. What suggestions do you have for people who do not bring their fair share of food to fellowship dinners?

5. Without being unduly critical, what is the biggest problem encountered at fellowship dinners in your church?

6. Give some creative ideas on how the work load entailed in planning successful fellowship dinners can be shared with more than the same faithful few.

7. Discuss some solutions to the problem of not having enough food to feed the multitude waiting to be fed at a fellowship dinner.

8. Share some ideas about the most successful fellowship dinners you have attended.

9. What can you personally do to make the fellowship dinners more successful? Are you willing to do it?

10. What rewards are promised to those who practice hospitality in Isaiah 58:6-10?

Lesson 7

HOSPITALITY AT HOME

1. Practicing hospitality at home. Read about the woman in Proverbs 31:10-31, noting how she practices hospitality at home.

   v. 13 _____

   v. 14 _____

   v. 15 _____

   v. 20 _____

   v. 21 _____

   v. 22 _____

   In what ways did the Proverbs 31 woman care for her family's emotional and spiritual needs as well as their physical needs?

2. Some verses in Proverbs give insight into how a hospitable and courteous spirit might work at home. Read and discuss how to apply the principles in each of the following verses.

Proverbs 15:17	Proverbs 21:9	Proverbs 23:3, 4
Proverbs 17:1	Proverbs 21:19	Proverbs 25:24
Proverbs 19:13b	Proverbs 23:2	Proverbs 27:15, 16

3. Dolores Curran in *Traits of a Healthy Family* states that healthy families "are very protective of the time allotted to the family dinner hour and often become angry if they're asked to infringe upon it for work or pleasure. A good number of respondents indicated that adults in the healthiest families they know refuse dinner meetings as a matter of principle. They discourage their children from sports activities that presume upon the dinner hour as a condition for team participation . . . and they never allow television to become a part of the menu."

   Is mealtime a priority in families you are acquainted with?

   Brainstorm some ideas for helping families in your church recognize the importance of the dinner hour and honor that time.

Share some creative ideas helpful in making mealtimes more pleasant.

a. For a married woman employed outside the home.
b. For a single mother.
c. For a single person.
d. For a full-time homemaker.

As a result of today's lesson, I will . . . _____

_____

A special touch that I will add to my family's next meal together will be . . . _____

BIBLIOGRAPHY

Aldrich, Joseph C. *Life-style Evangelism.* Portland, Oreg.: Multnomah Press, 1981.

Bailey, Lee. *Lee Bailey's Good Parties.* New York: Clarkson N. Potter, 1986.

Baldridge, Letitia, rev. *The Amy Vanderbilt Complete Book of Etiquette.* Garden City, N.Y.: Doubleday and Co., 1978.

Best Buffets. By the editors of *Better Homes and Gardens.* Meredith Pub. Co., 1963.

Brestin, Dee. *The Joy of Hospitality.* Wheaton, Ill.: Victor Books/SP Pub., Inc., 1993.

Bride's Lifetime Guide to Good Food and Entertaining. New York: Congdon and Weed, Inc., 1984.

Collier, Carole. *Serving Food With Style.* Garden City, N.Y.: Doubleday and Co., 1981.

Crocker, Betty. *Betty Crocker's Buffets.* 1st ed. New York: Random House, 1984.

Donnelly, Hallie, and Janet Kersel Fletcher. *Menus for Entertaining.* San Ramon, Calif.: California Culinary Academy, Chevron Chemical Co., 1988.

Entertaining for All Seasons. By the editors of Sunset Books and *Sunset Magazine.* Menlo Park, Calif.: Lane Pub. Co., 1984.

Green, Robert L. *Live With Style.* New York: Coward, McCann and Geoghegan, Inc., 1978.

Ladd, Karol. *Parties With a Purpose.* Nashville: Thomas Nelson.

LeFever, Marlene D. *Creative Hospitality.* Wheaton, Ill.: Tyndale House, Inc., 1980.

Mains, Karen B. *Open Heart—Open Home.* Elgin, Ill.: David C. Cook, 1976.

McCall's Book of Entertaining. New York: Random House, 1979.

Pittman, Grace. *Hospitality With Confidence.* Minneapolis: Bethany House, 1986.

Post, Elizabeth L. *Emily Post's Etiquette.* 14th ed. New York: Harper and Row, 1984.

Rose, Lennie. *Parties With Panache.* Chicago: Turnbull and Willoughby, 1986.

Sherrer, Quin, and Laura Watson. *A House of Many Blessings.* Ann Arbor, Mich.: Servant Publications, 1993.

Stoddard, Alexandra. *Daring to Be Yourself.* New York: Avon Books, 1990.

Williams, Milton. *The Party Book.* Garden City, N.Y.: Doubleday and Co., 1981.

Wills, Maralys. *Fun Games for Great Parties.* Los Angeles: Price, Stern, Sloan.